Mother-in-law

Daughter-in-law

Dilemma

Pamela Reynolds

DEDICATION

This book is dedicated with love

To my husband Paul J. Reynolds

Whose constant help, care

and loving support

is always evident.

"MY PRINCE CHARMING"

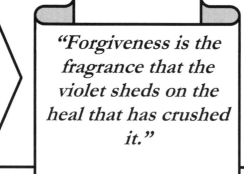

"Forgiveness is the fragrance that the violet sheds on the heal that has crushed it."

Mark Twain

CONTENTS

ACKNOWLEDGEMENTS

Dr. Emily Stanford
Marge Collette
Gina Latino
Doris Shannon
Sharon Woodman
Linda Cahill
Teresa Benoit
Mary Shannon
Dolores Ruffo
Helen Stroiney
Lisa Bergman
Carolyn Lagassie
Beth Crotty
Heather Colapinto
Doreen Brady
Nancy Hindes
Margaret O'Neill

Helen Haley
Babette Haley
Jen Bundy
Grace Benoit
Jill Nicholas
Gracie Benoit
Linda Cahill
Marge Collette
Suzanne Carlson
Judi Manfre
Carol Chatterton
Cathy Levesque
Cheryl Spencer
Dina Murray
Diane Kuzmeski
Shelley Cutter
Linda Tine

Beth Brown

I give thanks to numerous others, over the years, who wished to remain anonymous.

INTRODUCTION

There has always been controversy whenever the subject of mothers-in-law or daughters-in-law has generated a discussion. This issue seems to manifest silence, laughs, anger, jokes, ridicules, or a combination of all of these. There are no simple answers or elaborate solutions to this dilemma. There actually is no right or wrong partner. Both the mother-in-law and daughter-in-law lose when a balanced compromise has not been achieved. The purpose of this book is to help women find an emotional equilibrium in their lives, so that they might both be able to share the man they both love.

Perhaps with understanding, tolerance and acceptance will emanate. With tolerance and acceptance the barriers that both women construct, can be broken down so that a more enriching relationship will be fostered. Possibly this might allow both women the opportunity to enjoy each other's company and in the process, enable them to create their own relationship.

Reasonable adults are capable of logically placing matters into perspective when presented with all of the facts. Perhaps by seeing another point of view, we are given the opportunity to assimilate that viewpoint, and then accommodate it with our own perspective. Our uniqueness as individuals with our own personalities, allows us to undertake our own course of performance. It is perhaps, no small task to come to terms with each other's differentiations. It might call for a tremendous amount of effort in order to attain a profounder appreciation of and a genuine affection for each other. Many components perchance, can get overlooked by a substantial number of mothers and daughters-in-law.

Feasibly with knowledge, we might question our assumptions or conclusions more often, taking more time pursuing and analyzing our root of argument. Conceivably we might incorporate the feelings, and emotions at the time of the transgression, and fold them into the facts. Potential health considerations can feasibly be considered as well as money, age, and family responsibilities. The list continues and differs with each individual's circumstances. Each situation is likely to be distinct in certain circumstances yet universal in other respects.

The mistakes possibly begin almost from day one when our sons bring home a girlfriend. This visitor is for all accounts, a stranger to everyone in the family except the son. Although a stranger, the young woman is about to be placed in a position of honor as far as the young man is concerned. It is reasonable to assume the stress this creates for the future mother-in-law. It might be reasonable for the young woman to consider that although the family is presumed to embrace her, the family was not consulted, not to say they should have been, as to their desire to have her there in the first place. It appears likely that one should tread slowly and judge unhurriedly.

Families are expanded as infants are entered into the family. As each child enters into the family, it is gradually assimilated and accepted by other siblings and family members. When a son brings home another woman, it is reasonable to anticipate that all factions feasibly, must accept this newcomer who is about to become an instant family member. Obviously not nurtured within the family structure, nor influenced or persuaded towards the rest of the family's way of thinking, she possibly can be seen as a threat to the normal functioning within the family. It is reasonable to believe she has access to the private affairs, feelings and shortcomings of all of the family members. She conceivably gains all of this power, but does not yet have the emotional attachments to her future husband's family.

These circumstances are absolutely not the fault of the young woman. The problem arises when she potentially judges her future husband's family harshly before she creates any affection for them. Credibly the family history with all of its' pain and suffering probably is not a part of the young woman's experience. All of this missed emotional impact should conceivably suggest an abstaining of condemnations.

Our habits and opinions take years to develop. It warrants one to suspend quick disapprovals. One might reasonably delve beneath the surface of issues, and perhaps discover the origin of a person's habits and opinions. Siblings might recognize their family's shortcomings, but they are judging from a larger picture. Love is a part of their appraisal. The siblings see the goodness within their own families and they recognize their family's strong points. This enables people within a family to overlook the drawbacks. Most often a newcomer might conceivably be more critical.

The future daughter-in-law is at this point, in a vulnerable situation. She most likely wants to offer a good image. It is feasible that she is not at this point interested in the families past or in the family's problems. She might happen to feel in the middle regarding her position. It is possible that she perceives herself as meddling if she asks too many questions or unsympathetic if she does not get involved. Perhaps this control situation might possibly become a diplomacy situation. Potentially, dominance is a key word in the mother-in-law and daughter-in-law relationship. No matter who is wielding the power, it seems the outcome is inevitably loss for all involved. An avoidance of a day of reckoning down the road can be attained if caution is adhered.

The many mothers-in-law', daughters-in-law' pitfalls are avoidable. By being aware and taking the extra patience and time at the beginning of the relationship, possibly a mother-in-law and daughter-in-law can reconcile differences with a lot less conflict. This book will encourage both parties to reflect, analyze, assimilate and then accommodate their thoughts and emotions into a universalism that will allow for common ground. It is achievable for all to realize that with more understanding and patience life is a less complicated.

From the beginning, it is doable for mothers-in-law and daughters-in-law to refrain from drawing conclusions. The reader will be taken through 10 concepts. In each chapter there will be follow up stories, and questions for both the mothers-in-law and the daughters-in-law. Conceivably these stories and questions might help to generate, ideas and coping techniques.

This is an insightful, thought-provoking book, which invites female readers to think critically about the importance of the dynamic between mothers-in-law and daughters-in-law as well as to take a proactive approach to this relationship.

Mother-in-law Daughter-in-law Dilemma

1 CONTROL VS. DIPLOMACY

Evolving into our own person requires strength of character and confidence in our own abilities to make decisions. Others can unwittingly destroy the seeds of self-esteem planted within us. People assail mastery over others with or without consent. One must realize that with power comes responsibility. We teach children to include others and to share and take turns when they play, yet we, as adults, at times like to exclude others we don't deem desirable to our standards. We, as adults, hate to take turns. We like to perhaps have it, do it, make it, and force it our way. What we teach our children is what we need to emulate in our own behavior. Perhaps we need to ask ourselves where the other person's freedom is to choose and pick and do and make. It is probable that with more thought more freedom will automatically develop. Perchance, without having to actually wear another's shoes, we might reflect on what that would feel like. Social intelligence should be attainable if we think

> "There are two ways of exerting one's strength: one is pushing down, the other is pulling up."
>
> Booker T. Washington

and feel with the heart.

Force

> "Don't smother each other no one can grow in the shade."
>
> Leo Buscaglia

> "Real education should educate us out of self into something far finer; into a selflessness which links us with all humanity."
>
> Nancy Astor

Unchecked power and control may breed destruction of others. Having authority over another practically commands one to nurture and aid those we influence. Mothers-in-law likely have the ability to manipulate their sons. Wives feasibly have the ability to bias their husbands' beliefs. The man, who is caught in the middle of this power struggle, potentially remains the intermediary between his wife and mother. Neither woman should intentionally manipulate the man. Influencing does not equate to directing another. Freedom is always at the forefront of our dealings.

We may possibly venture to control others through fear or guilt. Either option may promote feelings of distrust. A person cannot function forever out of anxiety or self-reproach. Most often, mothers and wives are not aware of or thinking about the man they have in common. His feelings about any given situation conceivably are not taken into account. He will possibly suffer the wrath of whichever woman he scorns.

Decisions

Decision-making in a marriage ideally elects collaboration. An egalitarian marriage weaves honesty and respect. A mother-in-law's discretion in any arbitration between the couple is warranted. A couple's resolutions are confidential, with both partners participating equally. A wife must reasonably consider her husband an equal partner in the marriage and not just a likely puppet. A mother must reasonably consider and respect the fact that her son is capable of making his own decisions with his wife as they form their own household.

> *"The greatest of faults, I should say, is to be conscious of none."*
>
> *Thomas Carlyle*

Each household's business is private. Delving into another's confidential affairs is inconceivable. Privacy should always be considered a priority. Upon marriage, most couples set up their own household. This allows for a separation from both sets of parents. Separate living quarters constitutes viably detached transactions. A couple needs to trust each other and work together to make their situation successful. A solution to a problem is possible when a couple relies on each other's ability to resolve a problem. An achievable goal is the confidence that must enter into the couple's marriage.

Money

> "Love is as necessary to human beings as food and shelter; but, without intelligence, love is impotent and freedom unattainable."
>
> Aldous Leonard Huxley

Money, feasibly, might be used as a wedge or bartering tool. Money can be an authoritative weapon. It is difficult to compete with such an effective device. Money conceivably commands and enforces. Innocent people can easily get caught in its web. Money has the potential to promise, indulge, gratify, corrupt, and destroy. The worst thing that money achieves is the capability of influencing the way people respond. The attainable power of money is to motivate others for the benefit of one's own good. Reasonably, the person holding the wealth is the only winner. Most often, the use of money as leverage is compelling.

Love, as a tool, may potentially be used as a manipulator of power. A young man who is anxious to please his wife will be only too happy to say and do whatever it is she wants. If this unwittingly hurts the mother-in-law, the potential for disagreements is likely. The same young man, who has always placed his trust in his mother and allows her to influence his judgment, may unintentionally incense his wife, who perceives his decision as disloyalty to her. Most often, if a young woman is aware of her own parents' influence in her decision-making, it

> "People only see what they are prepared to see."
>
> Ralph Waldo Emerson

> *"Wear your learning, like your watch, in a private pocket; and do not pull it out and strike it, merely to show that you have one. "*
>
> Lord Chesterfield

might allow for lenience toward her mother-in-law's input. It seems that if a mother-in-law has trust and confidence in her son, this likewise should give her the confidence to let go and allow her son the freedom to make his own decisions.

The couple is a team and needs to work as such. Evidence suggests that when a young man coerces his mother into voicing an opinion and potentially agreeing with him, he has done a grave injustice to both his wife and his mother. Likely, this adds to the strain of the relationship.

1st Vignette

Abby was an only child. When she first met Adam, she was thrilled with his home life, which was a constant flurry of commotion. Adam was one of five siblings. Abby fell in love with Adam's whole family, and they loved her in return. The holidays inevitably caused the necessity of making emotional decisions. Adam believed there was never any compromise.

They always spent the holidays with Abby's parents. Abby believed she was bound to spend the holidays with her own family. Being an only child, she never even questioned the plan. Abby never realized the impact it was having on Adam. When the holidays approached, Adam got sullen, introverted, and uncoop-

> "He that never changes his opinions never corrects his mistakes and will never be wiser on the morrow than he is today."
>
> Edward Tryon

erative. Adam never outwardly complained because he perceived that Abby's parents, Alice and Henry, would be alone if he and Abby did not share the holidays with them.

Adam knew all of this in his heart, but it was heavy when he thought about his own family and the festivities. Despite his consent to spend the holidays with Alice and Henry, every year it was becoming more difficult to cope.

Adam was frustrated with his lack of input regarding where he and Abby spent the holidays. He felt helpless until, one year, Adam requested that they spend Thanksgiving with his family. Adam suggested they include Abby's parents as well.

The invitation was extended three weeks in advance to Alice and Henry. Abby and Adam were surprised when Abby's parents declined the invitation. When Adam and Abby confronted Alice, she mustered excuses, complaining about the car ride and her failing health. Abby questioned her mother about her health. Alice conceded that she'd been having some chest pain and some difficulty breathing. Alice confided to Abby and Adam that the doctor had scheduled her for various tests after the holidays.

> "He who angers you conquers you."
>
> Elizabeth Kenny, Australian Nurse

Abby sunk into the closest

chair, blankly staring out the window and biting her lips. Adam, who had been standing, stiffened his stance and refused to sit down at Henry's request. Adam glared at Alice and Henry as he stoically suffered defeat once again.

Henry interrupted the silence. "I think I should give you kids your holiday check early so that you can go shopping." Henry proceeded to write a check. With faltering steps, Henry gave Abby the check. Adam gritted his teeth and squeezed the chair top he was leaning on. The check was a ritual every Thanksgiving. Henry insisted Abby get the money early so that she could use it for holiday shopping. Adam wished they would just wait for the holiday like everyone else. Adam yanked his coat off the rack, tossing it over his shoulder without putting it on. Without a thank-you he shoved open the door and abruptly departed. With long quick strides, he reached his car door and yanked it as it slipped in his hands and released. He yanked it again harder, and the door swung opened as quickly as he slammed it shut. Abby expediently said her good-byes and raced in pursuit of Adam.

> "The degree of one's emotion varies inversely with one's knowledge of the facts. The less you know, the hotter you get."

Adam was furious and distressed. He and Abby fought all the way home. He refused to alter their decision to spend the holiday with his family. Abby was upset, confused, and in the middle. It wasn't that she disliked Adam's family or didn't want to spend the holiday with them. She could not see any other way to solve this problem. Abby prepared her speech to Adam and tossed the words from her lips in quick succession. Abby used the old argument that Adam's family had so many members that the two of them would hardly be missed. Adam exploded. He asserted he was not just one of a crowd, but an individual who counted with his family. He contended they were each missed at the holidays. Adam professed his displeasure. He explained his annoyance at what he perceived as Abby's ploy at dispensing guilt. Adam remained resolute. He was determined to spend this holiday with his family regardless of what Abby wanted.

> 'Make the best of what is in your power, and take the rest as it happens."
>
> Epictetus

Adam stated and affirmed the advancing ages of his own parents. Abby was unhappy, but she realized how important it was to Adam to share time with his family during the holiday season. Abby reasoned that she had few choices, given Adam's unhappy state of mind. She acquiesced and arranged to go to Adam's family for the holidays.

1st Discussion

Power and control dominate this conflict. Abby's parents rebelled against change. They were content to eliminate alternatives. By declining Adam's offer, they

> "The price of greatness is responsibility."
>
> Norman Vincent Peale

anticipated the coercion of the couple into canceling their plans.

Abby's parents might have been more cognizant of Adam's concerns. More contemplation and reflection could have fostered a more harmonious settlement. Abby might have expressed her distress to her parents long before it resulted in Adam's despair. Abby tried to command the situation using the old assertions against Adam to maintain constraints. The arguments did not achieve the usual results. Although Adam's parents had many members to share their celebration, they lamented Abby and Adam's absence. When Abby's attempts to convince Adam to spend the holidays with her parents were unsuccessful, she surrendered and deferred to Adam's wishes.

Adam obviously was harboring emotions of discontent for quite some time. Prior to reaching his limit of anger and exploding, an arrangement to discuss his sentiments might have been sanctioned with less disturbance and upset. Attainable communication should not be undervalued. It is reasonable to acknowledge the influence of group sanctioning and the resolution of issues. A couple might work on and achieve arbitration by respecting each other's wants and needs. True power and con-

> "Do not quench your inspiration and your imagination; do not become the slave of your model."
>
> Vincent Van Gogh

trol is fluid, open, and flexible.

2nd Vignette

Pat and George had two children, a six-year-old named Jamie and a four-year-old named Todd. Pat was a stay-at-home mother, but was recently feeling restless and anxious. Her husband's moaning about job layoffs at his company increased her edginess. George would come home from work, snatch the newspaper, and brood in front of the television set. His worrying affected his eating and heightened Pat's nervousness.

> "Courage is what it takes to stand up and speak; Courage is also what it takes to sit down and listen."
>
> Herbert V. Prochnow, and Herbert V. Prochnow Jr.

Pat resolved to get a job and contribute to the finances. Pat did not want her children in day care, so she approached her mother-in-law, Emily. Likely, Emily wanted to oblige, but was afflicted with an arthritic knee and seasonal asthma. Pat did not consider these adversities relevant. Pat trusted Emily's ability to care for the children, and Pat admired Emily's capability and boundless energy. Emily never complained, so Pat believed Emily would acquiesce and babysit.

Pat commenced, disclosing her fears to her mother-in-law. Pat justified her return to the work force as anxiety over George's possible job loss. This, she affirmed, was the motivating factor. Subsequently, Emily agreed to babysit. Pat located a job in a short while and proceeded to work. Emily was a disciplinarian and believed Pat was too easy with the children. Emily made it her mission to get the kids to behave. Pat was not happy with this arrangement, but felt helpless to speak her mind for fear of losing Emily as a babysitter. Emily took advantage of her situation and her empowerment and instilled her own rules and regulations with the children.

George suffered through several months of distress. Emily was delighted to be of help. Stability eventually returned to George's company. His job was no longer in jeopardy. It was unnecessary for Pat to continue working, but she enjoyed her new job. Pat refused to forsake her job. Emily's knee deteriorated, and her asthma worsened. Still, the babysitting arrangements remained.

Emily questioned George every day about curtailing her babysitting terms. George astutely avoided her queries when he picked the children up after work, and he habitually hustled the children out the door. Pat delivered the children to Emily in the morning, deliberately eluding conversation. Pat frowned at Emily's complaints, made excuses about her agenda, and rushed off to work.

Emily began to refuse all dinner invitations from Pat and George. Her bouts with asthma increased and her knee worsened, but she endured babysitting for her grandchildren.

2nd Discussion

Our needs prioritize our choices. These choices should not suppress or deprive the necessities of others. Consideration of humanity obliges us to reflect on the needs and wants of others.

Despite Emily's health problems, she accepted the job of caring for her grandchildren. It was difficult for Emily to ignore her son and daughter-in-law's request for help. Perhaps Emily did not consider that she was being manipulated, but she worried about being considered a mean mother-in-law if she refused to help. Conceivably, Emily also used the situation for her own advantage to discipline the children the way she saw fit. Emily didn't think about Pat's way of dealing with the children. Clearly, Emily has her own inhibitions to deal with here. The only recourse Emily has is to strongly state the conditions of her availability.

Manipulation can be powerful in controlling another. Pat subdued Emily and convinced her to adhere to the babysitting circumstances. Pat's agreement with Emily should have facilitated in Pat a responsibility toward her mother-in-law. The workable issue was for Emily to have had clear guidelines that related the restrictions and length of time her services would be required. It was doable for Emily to have regarded Pat's procedures for discipline as a priority. Pat's rules for the children should have been followed closely. Most often, Emily should have respected the fact that Pat was still the mother of the children instead of using Pat's need to work as an excuse to control her grandchildren.

When George's job was not precarious, Emily's liability to babysit should have ended. The conditions of the original agreement changed. This required renegotiations. The original crises situation Emily was presented with had changed and so her commitment to babysit should also have changed. A fluctuating situation should have reasonably allowed Emily to withdraw from babysitting when the emergency ended. Evidence suggests that Emily's lack of authority and expertise at articulating her needs produced ineffectual results. Resolutions are attainable with reasoning and logic as well as consideration of others. Final solutions do not guarantee complete satisfaction, but they might feasibly assure understanding and placation.

Reflections for Mothers-in-Law

Pay to have certain jobs done, if you can afford the money. It will save your son and daughter-in-law aggravation and an abundance of time.

Your son's responsibilities to his wife and children require your accommodation.

Patience and gratefulness is essential for any and all services provided by your son, as the time intervals he gives to you are taken from his wife and children.

Defer to your daughter-in-law's wishes to devote time to her own mother.

Using guilt as a tool to coerce your son lowers his effectiveness, concentration, and production.

Your son and daughter-in-law are capable of calculating and resolving their own dilemmas.

Credit your daughter-in-law's opinions, ideas, and thoughts on a multitude of subjects.

Reflections for Daughters-in-Law

Allowing your husband space is essential for his growth.

Your husband's family structure is established. Absorb it gradually, permitting it to absorb you.

Generate hospitality toward your mother-in-law, even with an unexpected visit.

Discuss issues openly with your mother-in-law. Differences of opinion foster greater opportunities to expand the mind.

Appreciate your mother-in-law's busy life when she declines to babysit.

Your husband possesses the capacity to love you *and* his mother.

Holidays should promote connectedness and enjoyment of each family member's presence. Arrangements made in advance may potentially enhance the holiday gatherings.

Evading faultfinding and criticism allows mothers-in-law and daughters-in-law to relish each other's company.

Questions for Daughters-in-Law

1. When your husband visits his mother, do you expect him home at a certain time?

   Always   Sometimes   Seldom

2. Do you rebel if your husband begins chores for his mother before he completes the jobs at home?

   Always   Sometimes   Seldom

3. When your husband is planning a visit to his mother who lives at a distance, do you alter the plans in any way?

   Always   Sometimes   Seldom

4. Do you mention the expense of a babysitter before asking your mother-in-law to babysit?

   Always   Sometimes   Seldom

5. Do you ever veto plans your husband makes with his mother?

   Always   Sometimes   Seldom

6. Do you like to know well in advance when your mother-in-law is coming to visit?

   Always   Sometimes   Seldom

7. Are you inflexible with last-minute changes of plans?

Always   Sometimes   Seldom

Questions for Mothers-in-Law

1. Do you keep an account of the gifts you buy for your son and daughter-in-law?

   Always   Sometimes   Seldom

2. Do you offer advice about decisions and plans your son and daughter-in-law have made?

   Always   Sometimes   Seldom

3. When you must wait for your son to complete a job for you, do you mention calling a specialist?

   Always   Sometimes   Seldom

4. Do you encourage your son and daughter-in-law who live at a distance to spend their vacation time with you?

   Always   Sometimes   Seldom

5. Do you allude to how long it's been since you have seen or heard from your daughter-in-law when she calls or comes to visit?

   Always   Sometimes   Seldom

6. Do you consider other lifestyles to be adverse?

   Always   Sometimes   Seldom

7. Do you like to choose the restaurant when you are going for lunch with your daughter-in-law?

   Always   Sometimes   Seldom

8. Are you inflexible with last-minute changes of plans?

   Always   Sometimes   Seldom

Mother-in-law Daughter-in-law Dilemma

2 INDEPENDENCE

The word *independent* conjures images of a self-determined, self-sufficient, unconventional, and self-reliant person. All of us have traits that are well developed and traits that need to be developed. We are unique individuals. We have our own way of doing and saying things. This, in many ways, makes us individualistic.

> "Listen to advice and accept instruction, and in the end you will be wise."
> Proverbs 19:20

There are so many colors of paint in the store and so many styles of furniture and houses. These colors and styles are a reflection of the various inclinations and partiality people exhibit. If stores recognize the limitless expressions of people, shouldn't we likewise be able to respect each other's various preferences?

Respect for each other's approach can carry over into every aspect of our lives. Some of us choose to dust our homes every other day while others choose to do it once a year. We do not have to live in each other's homes; we only visit each other's homes.

If a son and daughter-in-law choose to clutter their home, then they should be allowed to let clutter reign. If a mother-in-law chooses to have her home flawless, then that is her choice. Respecting our choices is respecting our uniqueness.

Generally, all mothers-in-law and daughters-in-law want to make a good impression on each other. Neither is anxious to irritate the other or cause problems. Conceivably, there is pressure on both women to say and do the correct thing.

> "We are not in a position in which we have nothing to work with. We already have capacities, talents, direction, missions, callings."
>
> Abraham Maslow

When a daughter-in-law tries too hard to say all of the suitable rhetoric, she runs the risk of saying too much or possibly appearing insincere. Some daughters-in-law are nervous and say too little, which can make them appear distant.

When we visit with our mothers-is-law, perhaps we are modifying ourselves in a variety of ways. This is natural.

Research shows that we all alter our role-playing according to the circumstances and the people we happen to be with at that time. Likewise, the impersonation we choose on a daily basis may vary.

Most often, the tone of voice and speech we adopt at work may be quite different from the tone and voice we elect to use at home. Likewise, our speech at home will be more relaxed.

All of the role-playing and role-changing displays a freedom that we all have. This liberty is important and necessary.

It appears that being independent does not mean that we must always be the person making commands. Perhaps if we are independent, then we are able to allow ourselves the indulgence of accepting help if we need it and refusing help if we do not. Feasibly maintaining control over our own lives is of the essence.

Allowing others to maintain control over their own lives is also relevant. When our son and daughter-in-law are visiting, we should allow for free expression. If we do not grant them freedom, then we may find them anxiously checking their watches to leave.

> "Nothing is so strong as gentleness, and nothing is so gentle as real strength."
>
> Ralph Sockman

It's promising to appreciate the fact that independence can mean many different things to a variety of people. To one couple, it might be expressed in the sharing of household tasks. Reasonably, to another couple, independence might connote that the woman has supervision of the house and children, while the man manages his career and the money. Neither individual infringes on the other.

One woman might sense that if she asks her husband for a favor, he will immediately grant it because she rarely asks. Another woman might conceivably be particular and have or share dominion with her husband. Each spouse might exhibit power and control in his or her own sphere of preference. Perhaps both parties are careful not to tread on each other's toes. Having the ability to judge people on their independence is therefore impossible.

A good rule of thumb might be if the couple is happy with the rules they have instituted, the marriage is working, and both husband and wife are happy, then they must be doing something right.

Consider what we envision when we buy a house. Likely, it is essential for some of us to have a garage, or a large kitchen, or an extra bedroom. We are making our own choices, and have no one to follow. Our criterion is different from others and defines us in such a way that our prerequisites can make us feel liberated and unique.

> " Ask yourself this question; "Will this matter a year from now?"
>
> Richard Carlson (writing in Don't Sweat the Small Stuff)

The way we choose to raise our children will be distinct. We have the ability and authority to manage our children in an adequate capacity. It happens that some women elect to stay at home and place their careers on hold, while other women elect to go back to work. Sending a child or children to day care is a distressful necessity. Likely, many women might be the sole providers, and they don't have the luxury of choice.

Being independent is being allowed to select a workable decision to continue with one's career or

> "Not in the clamor of the crowded street, not in the shouts and plaudits of the throng, but in ourselves are triumph and defeat."
>
> Henry Wadsworth Longfellow

stay at home with children. Mothers who stay at home might be frowned upon. Mothers who work feasibly may be offended by the reproach of others. Mothers-in-law must not judge their daughters-in-law's choices. Most of us have the choice of child rearing at some point in our lives, and we must do what is right for us.

Some husbands are more supportive than others and make returning to work easier. Other husbands leave the brunt of the childcare to the woman.

Whatever the circumstance, a mother may choose part-time work or take an absence from work. Each couple is an individual case, and their decisions are independent of another couple's resolutions. Independence is having the freedom to select what's best for us and to have those choices respected.

> "Thus each person by his fears, gives wings to rumor and without any real source of apprehension men fear what they themselves have imagined."
>
> Lucan

Sometimes being unconventional requires us to acknowledge the independence of another. This reasonably might compel us to acquiesce our desires for that of another.

Mothers have had complete access to their children through

all the years of child rearing. They might even continue to have this freedom of access even beyond college and into their adult child's first apartment. What most parents do not consider is the juncture when their adult children have significant others in their lives. At this stage, they need and want the freedom to live their own life. Perhaps privacy, rules, and scheduling become a necessity.

> "It is not work that kills men but worry. Work is healthy; You can hardly put more on a man than he can bear. But worry is rust upon the blade. It is not movement that destroys the machinery but friction."
>
> Henry Ward Beecher

The most difficult task now is for the mother, who has probably helped furnish and set up her child's household, to step back and basically back off. This is an almost insurmountable undertaking. Some think about how they had just been called upon for a simple recipe and repair issue, but now the freedom of communication is blocked. Stopping by for a quick visit perhaps becomes unquestionably not allowed.

Perhaps the daughter-in-law's mother does not have the same restrictions. One might question this logic. Understandably, the daughter-in-law does not want her mother-in-law's observations of the overflowing bucket, the overfilled laundry basket, the dirty dishes in the sink, or whatever the case may be.

> "God never made anyone exactly like you and He never will again."
>
> Norman Vincent Peale

It is necessary to be aware of the fact that we all deal with these same situations. It is probably best for all concerned to withdraw from comment. The more a mother-in-law doesn't "notice," the more likely she is to bring about a daughter-in-law who is at ease. There should be no guilt bestowed or insinuated. If the mother-in-law, however, chooses to recognize and acknowledge every carelessness she witnesses, she will most likely be relegated to scheduled, safeguarded invitations.

Evidence suggests that some mothers-in-law are consigned to scheduled visits even though they have carefully avoided any transgressions. Wary daughters-in-law are not yet willing to take the chance of allowing their defenses to be exposed.

Time and trust can be expanded over the years, building a more congenial relationship. When mothers-in-law stop without an invitation, they are infringing on their sons and daughters-in-law's independence. Likewise, when the daughter-in-law forbids her mother-in-law to ever stop by for a visit unless the visit is scheduled, she is also infringing on her mother-in-law's freedom to see her son. It is imperative for both women to realize

> "Few things are impossible to diligence and skill...great works are performed not by strength but perseverance. "
>
> Dr. Samuel Johnson

and accept this fact by cooperating with each other and allowing the relationship to move forward. Most husbands do not feel threatened by unannounced visits from their mothers-in-law; hence, the wife's mother is extended the courtesy of unscheduled visits. The husband's mother is perhaps seen as judgmental and more observant of household disarray. It is not important if this is truly the case or a subjective view of the daughter-in-law. What matters is how the daughter-in-law views visits from her mother-in-law.

Some mothers-in-law have made the mistake of jumping in to help their daughters-in-law with a mundane task. To their woe, they have been admonished. Conceivably, the mother-in-law feels she was only trying to assist, while the daughter-in-law likely sees this offer of assistance as a reproach to her incompetence. Perhaps many daughters-in-law like to feel they can handle anything. Perchance they have not yet reached the stage of being able to let go and allow support to be given. Research suggests that mothers-in-law are not thinking about incompetence. Most are recalling those difficult, stressful days when a lending hand was so welcomed. Daughters-in-law want their husbands to view them as efficient and capable individuals who have it all under control. At this point in their lives, mothers-in-law are more relaxed

> "Cruelty like any other vice requires no motives outside of itself; It only requires opportunity."
>
> George Eliot

and confident about child rearing because they have already been there and done that. Daughters-in-law, on the other hand, are learning as they go but want to appear confident on the outside, while dismissing any angst they have on the inside.

Nothing is more detrimental to a situation than having a daughter-in-law feel so overwhelmed by her mother-in-law that she conceivably feels she must deflate her mother-in-law by criticizing her or by criticizing the man she raised. A husband's bad habits can viably become the fault of his mother. The mother-in-law is seen as the person who raised him and made him messy, sloppy, and without any table manners. All the wonderful reasons that made this same woman want to marry him in the first place have been left astray. The mother-in-law is not given credit for his virtues, but only his vices.

> "In the depths of winter I finally learned that there was in me an invincible summer."
>
> Albert Camus

Mothers-in-law might be blamed for a whole array of things, such as his habit of eating too quickly, his dislike of vegetables, his love for candy, and any other baggage that might be added to this list. Both the mother-in-law and the daughter-in-law might reflect upon this criticism.

Conceivably, by berating her mother-in-law, a daughter-in-law lowers her own bar and feels less anxious about competing with her mother-in-law. Mothers-in-law must perceive the need to remain quiet and allow their daughters-in-law to blossom at their own rate. Never be critical. Allow your daughter-in-law to work things out until she is more secure in her self-worth and ready to let go and let others be helpful. This will only come without criticism.

Research shows that most mothers-in-law who attempted to do all the right things when bringing up children, admitted that it still did not ensure positive outcomes. Raising children and attending to one's marriage are daunting tasks, not taken lightly by anyone. More than they know, mothers-in-law and daughters-in-law are on the same page. Most mothers-in-law could probably admit to countless and insurmountable issues they had to deal with when they were raising their children. The majority report that it was the most difficult task to accomplish and one that never left them secure in the moment. This should guide every mother away from expressing a criticism or complaint against another, no matter what her generation.

> *Obstacles don't have to stop you. If you run into a wall, don't turn around and give up. Figure out how to climb it, go through it, or work around it."*
>
> *Michael Jordan*

1ˢᵗ Vignette

Beth remarked at the boldness of today's generation. "I wish I had their guts twenty-five years ago," she blurted. Upon further questioning, she confessed her anxiety during her children's baby and childhood years.

> "It isn't for the moment you are struck that you need courage, but for the long uphill climb back to sanity and faith and security"
>
> Anne Morrow Lindbergh

Beth was enmeshed in what was happening in the world around her. She laughed light-heartedly, and a twinkle in her eyes brought back a time long past when her children were very young. Beth chose to breast-feed at a time when it was not at all accepted by the general population.

Many pediatricians were not knowledgeable about how, when, and where to feed the baby. You were on your own, as Beth recalled. Her mother reluctantly accepted it, but her mother-in-law ostracized her. Beth had to go to a private room every time the baby needed to nurse.

There were constant remarks about the baby's weight gain and ability to thrive on breast milk alone. When the baby would cry, the remarks would fly: "He must not be getting enough to eat."

When the baby was hungry again a short while later, more disparaging words were said: "He must not be getting enough to eat." Beth was tired of hearing those words.

At times, Beth would go home and replay everything. She would then end up crying. It was an uphill battle. Every day she questioned if she was doing the right thing. The baby would appear to be so calm and relaxed after nursing. It was at those times Beth was sure she was doing the right thing.

At other times, when the baby would cry and fret, Beth wondered if she was doing anything correct. Her mother-in-law's constant barrage of unsupportive comments wore Beth's convictions. Being a new mother, she was unsure of herself.

One day, Beth decided she should stop breast-feeding. She tried, but the baby would not accept the bottle. He was used to the breast and was not about to give it up so easily.

Beth cried and began nursing him again. A friend had recently had a baby and was breast-feeding. Beth called this friend and sat down with her for a long talk. Beth gained a renewed sense of purpose and continued breast-feeding more successfully.

> *"Not flesh of my flesh nor bone of my bone, but still miraculously my own. Never forget for a single minute, you didn't grow under my heart but in it."*
>
> *Anonymous*

Beth spent little time at her mother-in-law's to avoid the negative remarks. The baby, Paul, was about two when Beth's husband made plans for them to visit overnight with his mother. Beth's second son was a few months old. Beth was nursing him with more confidence. She now considered herself a pro, and she knew that her first son thrived on breast milk.

The questioning of Beth's child-rearing practices carried over into her toilet training abilities as well. Beth did not feel the need to rush her children to toilet train. When her son was two and her second son had just been born, Beth successfully got her two-year-old trained. She had not pushed him, but he was willing and able. Beth's mother-in-law had stated many times that her sons had not been easy to train. She expected Beth to experience a difficult time when toilet training.

Beth was happy that Paul was toilet trained. It made it so much easier to have only one child to change. Paul was just two years old, but bright and attentive. Beth packed Paul's training pants so that he could put them

> *"Forgiveness is the final form of love."*
>
> Reinhold Niebuhr

on during the night. He had not had any accidents, but it was not her house or crib, and she did not want to take any chances.

Beth was not looking forward to the visit, but it was something her husband really wanted to do. They arrived at her mother-in-law's late at night. Beth swiftly got the baby ready for bed and then began tucking her two-year-old toddler into bed. Her mother-in-law, who was helping, panicked when Beth did not place a diaper on him. "He's only two; he'll wet the bed," she said. Beth answered in a relaxed manner that he would not wet the bed and that he was trained.

Nothing more was said, but the next morning when Paul, the two-year-old, began to cry to get out of bed, Beth's mother-in-law, Kathy, rushed to get him. Kathy quickly led him to the bathroom and helped him peel off the foot pajamas. Kathy could be heard from behind the bathroom door. "You didn't wet your pants," she said. Beth was on the other side of the door smiling. Kathy had made many references to her own sons' toilet training days and the difficulty they had getting toilet trained. Beth wished her mother-in-law had trusted her when Beth said that Paul was toilet trained.

> *"Do not think you are on the right road just because it is a well beaten path."*
>
> Anonymous

Beth now speaks in a more forgiving manner about this incident. It is apparent it was in the past and of no consequence to the present. Beth's only regret is that she didn't speak to her mother-in-law about it years ago instead of allowing it to erode their relationship.

1st Discussion

It is difficult for most of us to accept the fact that there are many ways to do things and all of them are okay. We use different roads to get to the same destinations, yet when we apply different methods to child rearing, we take offense to each other. We begin to believe that our method is the only correct method. Respecting an individual's right to do what he or she considers best is one of the hardest things for us to accept. There are many people who managed to become adults though the various parenting skills of their respective parents. Most of us probably do not know at what age we ate whole food or at what age we toilet trained or took our first steps. If we do know, we probably don't care. Making trivial things mountains will only separate us on either side of that mountain.

> "Energy and persistence conquer all things."
>
> Benjamin Franklin

2nd Vignette

Maggie sat up in the bed admiring her new daughter. Her husband, Jason, and mother-in-law, Trish, were at her side. Maggie was beaming. She had such a hard time getting pregnant that she thought they would never have children. She was ecstatic as she handed her baby, Elise, to the nurse.

After the nurse took Elise to the nursery, Maggie confronted Trish with a question. She asked Trish if she could babysit two days out of the week.

Trish was astounded. Her face flushed. Trish had just assumed that Maggie would stay at home with the baby for a little while. Trish reluctantly agreed, but she was noticeably shaken and upset. Her brand new granddaughter was going to be in day care. Trish could hardly believe it. She was so fond of Maggie. It was Maggie who had nursed her through her own surgery a couple of years back. Maggie was so strong. She did her own thing, as Trish loved to say.

> "And the wind said...may you be as strong as the oak, yet flexible as the birch; may you stand tall as the redwood, live gracefully as the willow; and may you always bear fruit all your days on this earth."
>
> A Native American prayer

How could Maggie just go back to work and leave her young daughter? Trish shook her head as she looked at her son, Jason, who sheepishly glanced back at his wife.

Trish argued with Jason all the way home. She made it a point that she'd stayed at home with him. Jason gripped the wheel of the car and tensed his body. He wished his mother would just be quiet. His wife, Maggie, had made a decision. Jason knew that when Maggie made up her mind, it was like a brick

> "I believe in getting into hot water; It keeps you clean."
>
> G. K. Chesterton

wall.

Maggie decided to go right back to work, and that was what she was going to do. Maggie worried about money all of the time. They had more than enough, but Maggie had already planned on opening a bank account for Elise.

Maggie grew up without a father, and her own mother had gone back to work out of necessity. Maggie feared being destitute. She wanted to guarantee that Elise would never have to worry about being poor. Maggie trusted Trish and was confident Elise would be in exceptional hands. Jason understood Maggie's fears to a point, but he believed she was overreacting a bit. He did not admit this to his mother, as he thought it best to keep quiet.

Jason brought his mother home and begged her to keep her feelings to herself. Trish grumbled as she got out of the car. It was easy for Jason to say, but he wasn't going to be the one doing the babysitting.

Jason rode home alone questioning his wife's decision. His mother and his wife were both strong-willed. He wasn't sure who was right or wrong. Jason was confused and agitated. He only wanted the best for his daughter. His mother always thought she had all of the right answers. Now all Jason could

> "A man who removes a mountain begins by carrying away small stones."
>
> Chinese Proverb

> *"Day by day, nothing seems to change, but pretty soon, everything is different."*
>
> *Calvin and Hobbes (comic strip)*

think about was Maggie's decision to go back to work.

Jason tossed and turned all night and was extremely tired the next day. He dressed, ate, and left for the hospital. He prepared his argument with Trish as he drove. Jason was tense and confused when he parked his car and climbed out of it. Jason could not get his mother's remarks out of his head. He really did not want to argue with Maggie, but his mother's theories continued to play in his mind. He entered Maggie's room and stood stiffly by her bedside. There was no hint of a smile, just a blank stare from Maggie. As Maggie tipped her head and wrinkled her eyebrows, Jason blurted out that maybe she should stay at home with the baby for a while. Maggie frowned and then laughed. "You've been talking to your mother," she said. Maggie and Jason talked for hours. Jason's fears were somewhat allayed, but he was still not convinced Maggie's decision was the right one. Maggie was inflexible. Jason would have to accept Maggie's decision and lay his mother's fears to rest.

> *"Nothing splendid has been achieved except by those who dared to believe that something inside them was superior to circumstance."*
>
> *Bruce Barton*

2nd Discussion

Questioning each other's choices appears to be everyone's job. Maggie has made a decision that is right for her. It is her decision. Jason may give his input, but Maggie has made a resolution that is right for her. Although on the surface this appears to be no concern of the mother-in-law, she is ultimately the one who will be doing the babysitting. Trish needs to allow this couple to make their own evaluations and then she can select to babysit or decline the offer. The couple is content with their decision, and Trish should not be undermining the choices they have made. Jason is left with doubts. The world changes, times change, people change, jobs change, and society changes. A new generation has its own ideas on many subjects.

Trish pressured the couple by interfering with a shared decision. Until Trish voiced her concerns, Jason was content with Maggie's choice. The time and circumstances were different when Trish was at home with Jason. It is not a good thing for a woman to stay at home with her children if she is not satisfied. It will be detrimental to the children. If the mother is unhappy and depressed and anxious, her ability to nurture well will be in jeopardy. If a mother is forced

> "Your life is something opaque, not transparent, as long as you look at it in an ordinary human way. But if you hold it up against the light of God's goodness, it shines and turns transparent, radiant and bright."
>
> Albert Schweitzer

> "Use what talents you possess; the woods would be very silent if no birds sang except those that sang best."
>
> Henry Van Dike

to return to work against her desires, she will also be unhappy, anxious, and depressed, and this will affect her work. It appears to be so difficult for us to accept people for who they are. We cannot make each other enjoy the things that we enjoy. We cannot change our attitudes, personalities, or characters. We can only be what we are and allow others the same freedom.

Reflections for Mothers-in-Law

Allow your daughter-in-law free speech. Correcting or criticizing will keep her from voicing her feelings and opinions. This will be detrimental to all. Variety in a soup is what makes it interesting; this idea should be applied to life.

Your son and daughter-in-law's plan for a working relationship may be very different from the one you and your husband chose. Accept this difference graciously.

The choices your daughter-in-law makes for child rearing may contrast with the methods you used. Your grandchildren will grow and thrive mentally, physically, emotionally, and socially.

Approaches to housecleaning and spending are a personal matter. Allow it to remain personal.

Exhibiting a reproachful attitude will cause your daughter-in-law to defend herself, possibly in a disrespectful manner.

Applaud your daughter-in-law's efforts to be successful.

Many of our diverse attitudes and values are the result of the diverse homes of origin.

Allow your daughter-in-law to have friendships

and experiences that are apart from her commitments to you. It is important for everyone to have friends.

A married couple has the right to discuss and conclude a plan of action without input from outside sources.

Reflections for Daughters-in-Law

When you have chosen any course of action, assert yourself and follow through with your plans.

It is all right to be wrong and to make mistakes. Learn from your mistakes and continue to choose your own course.

Reflecting on what others say is a benefit, but, in the end, your decisions must reflect what is best for your situation.

Never fear to state your opinions even if they differ from your mother-in-law.

A new way for doing things does not necessarily make it better.

Your modus for raising children will be outdated in the near future. Remember to respect your mother-in-law's outdated methods.

Being independent is being able to admit that someone else might be right.

Being independent is not fearing being wrong.

Keep any disputes your husband has with his mother between him and his mother.

Questions for Mothers-in-Law

1. Do you challenge your daughter-in-law's opinions?

   Always   Sometimes   Seldom

2. Would you approve of your daughter-in-law's quick return to work after the baby is born?

   Always   Sometimes   Seldom

3. Does your daughter-in-law work to have more material possessions?

   Always   Sometimes   Seldom

4. Do you question any new method for doing things?

   Always   Sometimes   Seldom

Questions for Daughters-in-Law

1. Do you ever agree to something in order to keep the peace?

   Always   Sometimes   Seldom

2. Have you doubted decisions you have made?

   Always   Sometimes   Seldom

3. Are you usually able to convince your mother-in-law she is wrong?

   Always   Sometimes   Seldom

4. Are your decisions influenced by others' opinions?

   Always   Sometimes   Seldom

5. Would it bother you if your two-year-old was not toilet trained?

   Always   Sometimes   Seldom

Mother-in-law Daughter-in-law Dilemma

3 HOLIDAYS & GIFTS

Holiday time is stressful for everyone. Our expectations are high, and the majority of people are inescapably disappointed when the holidays fail us. Television and the media present us with images of happy, sentimental scenes. They forget to add sleep deprivation, headaches, fussy babies, broken homes, loss of life, sickness, job loss, disagreements, sadness, confusion, distrust, and lack of focus or direction.

> "The game of life is a game of boomerangs. Our thoughts, deeds and words return to us sooner or later with astounding accuracy."
>
> Florence Scovel Shinn

We have limited command of our lives, and the holidays constrain us even more. Recognizing the pitfalls of the holiday season does not ensure that all family members will have a wonderful day. It is essential that everyone make his or her own enjoyment. We cannot please others. We cannot be held responsible. When in-laws are a component to be considered, the anxiety is intensified. Recognizing the added burden of the holidays may help to alleviate the pressure of contending with in-laws.

Where to Spend the Holiday

Most couples facilitate discussions, conflicts, and arguments about where to spend an upcoming holiday. Those who live at a distance must weigh traveling plans. This compounds the anxiety and added distraction of organizing and packing. The mother-in-law may have other children to take into account. Perhaps the daughter-in-law wants to visit her own family. When a couple is still in the discussion stage of the decision, all the facts should be contemplated.

Once a resolution has been made, the plans are constructed and the work completed. When men agree with their wives' arrangement, peace and harmony are promoted.

"Don't forget the small kindnesses and do not remember the small faults."

Chinese proverb

It might appear irresponsible of the husband to remain neutral, but if compliance results in a peaceful holiday, then, conceivably, this is a troubleshooting solution. The problem will likely arise again and again without any magical remedy, and friction between the mother-in-law and daughter-in-law may intensify.

A new mother-in-law might put in more effort at securing her son and daughter-in-law's attendance for a holiday, only to learn that seeing them at some point during the holiday season is better than not seeing them at all.

Research suggests that most daughters-in-law reserve the first-place position for their own mothers while their mothers-in-law accept second place graciously. Feasibly, there is no other compromise that works. Understanding the dynamics helps everyone. Is this fair? Is there a better solution? The answers are difficult to grasp and likely the questions are ignored.

Most mothers-in-law are happy to be included even if it means second best. Any attempt at coercion by the mother-in-law is not suitable and might only advance future friction.

It is possible that a later dinner date will be more enjoyable and relaxed. Most often, this is not really about winning or losing for mothers-in-law, but how best to have the chance to spend time with their sons and their sons' wives.

> "Be glad of life because it gives you the chance to love and to work and to play and to look at the stars. The best rosebush after all is not that which has the fewest thorns but that which bears the finest roses."
>
> Henry Van Dyke

Visiting

Whatever the issues, couples have a difficult time deciding where they will attend a holiday celebration. We all search for time to spend with our own families, and trying to schedule time with in-laws can become a battleground. If there is fighting between the couple prior to the visit, it will be reflected in the attitudes the couple displays.

Some parents pressure their children to spend the holidays with them. If the son or daughter-in-law is from a smaller family, it might confuse the proceedings even more. If the husband or wife is an only child, it will also muddle the outcome.

"Fear less, hope more, eat less, chew more, whine less, breathe more, talk less, say more, hate less, love more, and good things will be yours. "

Oliver Goldsmith

When siblings live at a distance and cannot be counted on to entertain their parents, then this will also influence a couple's judgment. They may feel compelled to accept the burden and entertain their parents or be present at their parents' house. The couple has probably discussed this issue and come to an agreement, but the mother-in-law is not privy to the discussion. Tenably nothing might be said but considerable is assumed. What the husband's thoughts are about a given situation may not be considered.

> *"Remember this: whoever sows sparingly will also reap sparse, and whoever sows generously, also reaps generously."*
>
> Corinthians 9:6

It's possible that a daughter-in-law wants to spend time with her mother-in-law, yet she totally understands her commitments to her family are undisputable. By now we have an exhausted couple, most likely with erupting tempers.

The optimal circumstances are those that are the fairest, but fairness is potentially thrown out the window when complications arise. A good compromise is essential but not reasonably executed as often as it should be.

When Daughters-in-Law Visit

Those daughters-in-law who venture to spend the holidays with their mothers-in-law have their own worries and anxieties. They are conceivably saddled with fears of being crushed, ignored, and controlled. When a daughter-in-law brings her pets, it can place a burden on the mother-in-law. She may want to see her son and grandchildren so badly that she accepts these circumstances, which are an added encumbrance.

> *"Wherever there is a human being, there is an opportunity for kindness."*
>
> Seneca

Daughters-in-law may discount the amount of paraphernalia that accompanies them when they are visiting. Many daughters-in-law dismiss the fact that they are not in their own homes, and they do not always consider the baby's items as an intrusion on their mothers-in-law or their home. A living room may serve as a nursery, and a cherished coffee table may be used for food, bottles, and diapers. A mother-in-law's home becomes completely disrupted, but a mother-in-law's complaints might be viewed as disinterest in her grandchild or grandchildren.

> "We live in deeds, not years, in thoughts, not breaths; In feelings, not in figures on a dial. We should count time by heart throbs. He most lives who thinks the most-feels the noblest-acts the best."
>
> Philip James Bailey

Research suggests that most mothers-in-law will put up with just about anything to spend time with their grandchildren. They will probably work around a baby's schedule or a toddler's wants and needs. It really is important to respect your mother-in-law's items. By simply requesting where you might change the baby or feed the messy toddler, you are exhibiting an appreciation that might be what your mother-in-law was seeking. Adoring her grandchildren doesn't mean a mother-in-law will appreciate a complete lack of respect.

Likewise, if a daughter-in-law is apprehensive when she needs to be excused from the dinner table to take care of a baby or toddler's needs, in the future she will greatly consider before accepting another dinner invitation. It is practicable for a mother-in-law to recall

> *"If ignorance is bliss, we should have a great many more happy people."*
>
> *Anonymous*

the busy, disruptive years of raising children.

When Mothers-in-Law Visit

A mother-in-law might elect to spend the holidays with her son and daughter-in-law, while a daughter-in-law might potentially be compelled to accept the arrangements.

Husbands need to become more involved when their mothers are visiting. It is honorable for them to contribute to their mothers' comfort and to assist their wives with the arrangements and workload. It is beneficial for the wives to affirm their expectations and accept help from their spouses and guests.

Mothers-in-law who live at a distance require overnight accommodations. Sharing close quarters may result in unexpected occurrences, which, evidence suggests, heightens the tension.

Mothers-in-law may bring a pet, which very likely brings compounded stress and confusion. A daughter-in-law may unwillingly accept a mother-in-law's pet because saying no to the pet could exacerbate the tension between the mother-in-law and daughter-in-law or force the mother-in-law to stay home. Acquiescing to the presence of pets realistically produces

> *"No act of kindness, no matter how small is ever wasted. "*
>
> *Aesop Greek fablelist*

additional work for the daughter-in-law. It also affords its own assemblage of complications. This is a viable situation if your pet is restrained, trained, and gentle with the children. If a pet is none of the above, it will need to be confined and definitely not allowed near the children. Pets should not freely roam another's home. Your daughter-in-law's home is no exception, no matter how willing and accommodating she might be.

When visiting your grandchildren, make an effort to dwell on the positive. If you are hypercritical, they might distance you from their lives. Make a reasonable attempt to overlook any annoying acts.

> "Most human beings have an almost infinite capacity for taking things for granted."
>
> Aldous Huxley

Another consideration when we have guests from out of town is that they may bring a traveling companion. A mother-in-law may have a close male or female friend who accompanies her. This presents a predicament concerning the sleeping arrangements. If there are young children involved, a mother-in-law's discretion is imperative so her grandchildren are not receiving mixed messages. This person may be a close friend to the mother-in-law, but is practically a stranger to the rest of the family. Overcoming these dilemmas can be demanding. Appreciating the compassion one's daughter-in-law displays in such situations should not be undervalued.

Children complicate the situation in other ways.

> *"Our dignity is not in what we do, but what we understand."*
>
> *George Santayana*

Grandparents want to see the children at holiday times, and they have the potential to induce the couple's compliance.

Gift Giving

Holiday gift-giving can set off a nightmare. Gifts may propose affection, gifts can be those effects we receive but don't really need, and gifts might have been presumed to be unique. Most often, the gifts we might select for ourselves are never the gifts we receive; therefore, we are certain to be disappointed. It is imperative that we realize these were gifts and not something we chose. Thinking of gifts as contemplated, abstract ideas may alleviate dissatisfaction. It is feasible that our gifts to others are as much of a disappointment to the receiver as their gifts were to us. Most often, people purchase items they themselves would value. What we cherish is not necessarily what others treasure.

Studies suggest some daughters-in-law refuse to purchase anything for their mothers-in-law. They buy for their own mothers and expect their husbands to do the same. Sometimes this rationale is workable. At times, this is not doable because men do not always go shopping. Gifts constitute affection to the receiver,

> *"You give but little when you give of your own possessions. It is when you give of yourself that you truly give."*
>
> *Kahil Gibran*

> "People love others not for who they are, but for how they make us feel. "
>
> Irwin Federman

and if the gifts are not yielding sentiment, then the way in which a gift is selected must be reconsidered.

Gifts are not vouchers to be used at a later time, and it is not a competition in scrutinizing the largest, most expensive gift. A gift reflects fondness and perhaps implies attention to and warmth for someone.

Sometimes a gift may appear thoughtless and clueless but stems from the heart. We should accept all gifts with gratitude. We must trust the gifts were credibly given in good faith. When you are acquiring a gift, reflect on what the receiver prefers for herself. Mothers-in-law and daughters-in-law would do well to avoid judging the gift by the price tag.

Gifts of time are the most valuable gifts. The small, thoughtful things that we say and do for each other are what counts. If your mother-in-law is constantly helping you out with the dog and children as well as inviting you for meals, she is no doubt worthy of your recognition. If your daughter-in-law stops to visit, invites you for dinner, runs an errand, or asks you to lunch, consider yourself favored. The gift of oneself is the most generous gift we have to give. It is underestimated,

> "Kindness is more important than wisdom, and the recognition of this is the beginning of wisdom. "
>
> Theodore Isaac Rubin

undervalued, and scarcely given freely. When receiving the gift of time, studies suggest many people forget to say thank you.

In summary, you can never be sure of the sincerity of the giver or the gift. Attempting to judge it is impractical. Trusting the promising gesture meant by the giver appears to be the best course of reaction.

1st Vignette

Stephanie was married to Steve. They had no children. Stephanie came from a large family and loved to cook. Her house was organized and clean at all times. Stephanie enjoyed sewing and needlepoint as well as all kinds of crafts. Stephanie consistently invited friends and family to dinner. She set her table with matching color and décor. It was an experience to have dinner at her house.

> "Love begins at home, and it is not how much we do... but how much love we put in that action."
>
> Mother Theresa

Stephanie's mother-in-law, Karen, hated to cook. She bought frozen meals and opened canned vegetables. The extent of her cooking was a burger in the frying pan. Karen was thrilled whenever Stephanie invited her for dinner. Stephanie enjoyed cooking for her mother-in-law and invited her to dinner often. Karen always remarked how delicious Stephanie's homemade bread tasted. One day, Stephanie made a mental note to purchase a breadmaker for her mother-in-law.

> *"That best portion of the good man's life-his little namelessness, unremembered acts of kindness and of love."*
>
> *Wadsworth.*

On Mother's Day, Stephanie had the opportunity to present her mother-in-law with a breadmaker. Stephanie anticipated an ecstatic reaction from her mother-in-law. Karen opened the gift and flashed angry glares at everyone. Karen was dissatisfied and harsh in her negative remarks to Stephanie. Karen shoved the gift back into the box and rigidly handed it to Stephanie. Karen questioned Stephanie about her reasoning for purchasing the gift.

Although Stephanie attempted to recite her arguments, Karen was resistant to all Stephanie had to say. Karen ceased all discussion and petitioned Stephanie to return the gift. Karen interpreted the breadmaker as rude. She even suggested that Stephanie keep the gift for herself.

Stephanie was crushed. She was deeply aware of how hurtful her gift appeared to be. Stephanie deduced how much her mother-in-law hated to cook. Stephanie concluded her mother-in-law could still have homemade bread by tossing ingredients into the machine. It required little effort, Stephanie thought. Stephanie was left without any options. The next week, she returned her mother-in-law's gift. Both women were discouraged and un-

> *"Be not overcome with evil but overcome evil with good."*
>
> *Romans 12: 21*

happy. Their once solid relationship now had some cracks.

1st Discussion

It was clear that Stephanie enjoyed cooking and would relish any kitchen object she received. The mistake Stephanie implemented was buying Karen something she would have liked to obtain herself. Stephanie's aim was for her mother-in-law to enjoy homemade bread even when her mother-in-law did not take pleasure in cooking. Stephanie aspired to save her mother-in-law the time and effort involved in bread-making, yet reward her with delicious results.

> *"Life is simply time given to man to learn how to live. Mistakes are always part of learning. The real dignity of life consists in cultivating a fine attitude towards our own mistakes and those of others."*

Karen did not see Stephanie's point of view. Karen assessed Stephanie's purchase as thoughtless. Karen assumed that if Stephanie had considered her needs, she would have recalled that she was not a cook or a baker. Stephanie did not anticipate the effect of the offering. Neither woman was able to communicate her thoughts about the gift. Both women were deeply wounded.

Before giving the machine to her mother-in-law, Stephanie might have explained the simplicity of using the appliance and procuring the benefits. This might have allayed Karen's fears in operating the mechanism.

It is most important to consider what behavior a person exhibits toward us more than a token gift they give to us. The intangible demeanor may reflect the inner feelings more than the tangible souvenirs.

2nd Vignette

> "How far you go in life depends on your being tender with the young, compassionate with the aged, sympathetic with the striving and tolerant of the weak and the strong. Because someday in life you will have been all of these. "
>
> George Washington Carver

Lori was thirty years old with short dark hair and a quick smile. Lori relished entertaining guests. It did not surprise Kyle, her husband, when she frequently invited the next-door neighbors. Kyle was accustomed to Lori's spur-of-the-moment gestures.

Lori came from a large family. She had four brothers and two sisters. Kyle had three siblings. At holiday time, both of their respective families yearned to have them at the dinner table. Lori and Kyle lived within two hours of both sets of parents, but it was frustrating and impossible to journey to two homes on the same day when they had to manage a two-hour drive.

When Lori and Kyle were first married, they agonized over what to do every time there was a holiday.

Lori was determined that she and Kyle not fight about where to spend the holidays.

One day, Lori suggested to her mother that they celebrate the holidays the week after the calendar holiday. At first, this sounded a little strange. Lori's siblings questioned the feasibility of it functioning, but they all resolved to give it a try. The suggestion turned into a regular yearly happening. It was still effective after ten years. Lori's family was satisfied with the situation. It allowed them the freedom to visit with their in-laws on the holidays without any hassles. Lori's family celebrated together after the holiday in peace and quiet. It was one of the best things they had ever achieved. If any members of the family had no place to go on the day of the holiday, they were welcome to enjoy two days of celebration, one on the day of the holiday and one the week later.

> "I expect to pass through life but once. If therefore, there be any kindness I can show or any good thing I can do to any fellow being, let me do it now and not defer or neglect it, as I shall not pass this way again."
>
> William Penn

They had a wonderful time and on no account was pressure applied. Lori, and her in-laws and her siblings' in-laws were quite gratified with the arrangement, which permitted them to plan their own celebrations. Lori and Kyle succeeded in eliminating holiday demands.

2nd Discussion

Lori admired her mother-in-law, and she welcomed being able to share two holidays. Lori and Kyle blended their families and came out ahead. Lori empowered everyone. The compromise had a satisfying effect on all. Sometimes the solutions are simple. Occasionally, there are no answers, and we must deal with whatever transpires. At other times, a daughter-in-law's own family might facilitate disagreements between the couple.

In Lori and Kyle's situation, Lori championed a decision. This resulted in arbitration with her parents. The circumstances were not ideal, but negotiating a compromise produced an equitable resolution.

Engaging everyone's participation to achieve a reasonable outcome for all promotes satisfaction. Evidence suggests harmony precedes love. Being a bigger person requires compromise.

Reflections for Mothers-in-Law

Remember your daughter-in-law has a family, too. She cherishes spending time with them.

Holidays remind us of past memories, which can be both good and bad. Keep the present holiday central, and be thankful to share it with people you love.

Your daughter-in-law may anticipate visiting her family on the holidays. She might be more anxious to see them if they live at a distance.

Try to give of yourself. When all is said and done, we remember who did what for us quicker than who gave what to us.

It is fun to visit with someone throughout the year. The holidays are only a short period of time. It is the people who make the holiday special.

You cannot compete with your daughter-in-law's mother. You can become a significant ally to your daughter-in-law.

Each holiday is unique in itself. It is not possible or necessary to repeat a holiday experience. Embrace each holiday. They have their own distinct moments.

Give unconditionally, and you will not be disappointed.

Equating the gifts from your daughter-in-law to the value she places on your worth is a mistake. Most of us choose a gift we would prefer for ourselves and one we can afford.

If your daughter-in-law starts her own holiday traditions, accept these changes graciously. Changes are a part of life. Join in the festivities.

Reflections for Daughters-in-Law

Lend a helping hand when possible, and remember to value the person who donates his or her time and effort for you.

Make an effort to visit with your mother-in-law at other times during the year. This is especially important if you do not get to spend the holidays with her.

Remember to cherish your mother-in-law's traditions. They were developed over numerous years and possess profuse memories.

Be fair in dividing your time and your husband's with your respective families. Your mother-in-law deserves equal attention.

Invite your mother-in-law for a holiday as you would your own mother. She is your husband's mother.

Do not equate your mother-in-law's gifts to how she cherishes you.

Do not anticipate quantity from your holidays or from your gifts. Search for quality.

Accept your mother-in-law's invitations to holiday meals whenever you are able.

Your family's traditions and your husband's family traditions will differ. Accept and rejoice in these differences.

Believe that love is shared and celebrated every day, not just on a holiday.

Questions for Mothers-in-Law

1. Are you supportive when your son and daughter-in-law share a holiday with her family?

   Always   Sometimes   Seldom

2. Do you refrain from complaining about your daughter-in-law's gift and consider the positive motives she might have had?

   Always   Sometimes   Seldom

3. Are favors you do for your daughter-in-law without obligations to you?

   Always   Sometimes   Seldom

4. Are you willing to change any of your traditions if it results in peace?

   Always   Sometimes   Seldom

5. Do you place as much importance on sharing a summer day with your son and daughter-in-law as you do sharing a holiday with them?

   Always   Sometimes   Seldom

Questions for Daughters-in-Law

1. Do you control your emotions when your mother-in-law invites you for a holiday three months in advance?

   Always   Sometimes   Seldom

2. Do you accept your mother-in-law's gifts in good faith, even if you do not like them?

   Always   Sometimes   Seldom

3. Are you aware of and value your mother-in-law's traditions, no matter how ridiculous they appear to you?

   Always   Sometimes   Seldom

4. Do you ever spend a holiday with your husband's family?

   Always   Sometimes   Seldom

5. Do you ponder the gifts you buy for your mother-in-law with care?

   Always   Sometimes   Seldom

4 MONEY

Money is vital to our survival. It can be used to influence, control, and multiply material possessions. Money may also contribute to arguments, contention, desire, envy, unhappiness, yearning, power, control, and guilt.

> "Not he who has much is rich, but he who gives much."
>
> Erich Fromm

People spend their childhood years growing up in homes where there are various amounts of wealth. Some people are more fortunate than others. Because of this and other variables, the gifts we like to give and the gifts we like to receive may differ. Many of us may be disappointed with the gifts from our mothers-in-law. We tell ourselves their presents lacked thought, but we might really be thinking they lacked an expensive price tag.

> "I have learned from experience that the greater part of our happiness or misery depends on our dispositions and not on our circumstances."
>
> Martha

Some parents have more money and resources and may want to give their children as much as they can for as long as they can. This does not mean parents must give any of their wealth to their children. They are not obligated. A mother-in-law should understand that even if she bestows a substantial amount of money on her son and daughter-in-law, the appreciation might never manifest more than a simple thank-you. One should never give a gift with any thought of being compensated for it. Reciprocation is not likely in your son or daughter-in-law's plan.

As long as a mother-in-law is aware that this is the situation, she should not be disappointed if there is no gratitude given. She needs to be reasonable regarding her possible expectations if her gift of money is accepted.

> "A part of kindness consists in loving people greater than they deserve."
>
> Joseph Joubert
> French philosopher

Predictably, if this is kept in perspective and the young couple can see the transformation of any links the gift might have to an unseen, but expected obligation, then everyone can and should benefit. There ought to be no strings attached. Love does not make us duty bound

> "Everything has its wonders, even darkness and silence, and I learn whatever state I may be in, therein to be content." "The best and most beautiful things in the world cannot be seen or even touched. They must be felt within the heart."
>
> *Helen Keller*

and cannot be bought.

If a mother-in-law can and is willing to offer monetary means to a couple in need, she should do so with no debt attached, unless all parties involved have a signed agreement. It is important, and recommended, that the couple exhibit appreciation for the support, even if they will be reimbursing the mother-in-law. The mother-in-law should not feel ashamed for having the affluence to help the couple financially.

It is essential to take pleasure in possessions that are not costly, especially if money is a problem. Money does not have to become a dispute. If it becomes a necessity to borrow money from your mother-in-law, it is essential to be prepared and arrange for the emotional cost. Will you have to respond to her every impulse? Will you think that you have to answer to her every notion? Will this debt be one that continues to haunt you throughout your lives?

> "A man who has taken your time recognizes no debt, yet it is the only debt he can never repay."
>
> *Papyrus*

A mother-in-law must be prepared for the possibility that her money may not be spent in a manner that she deems appro-

"I can live for two months on a good compliment."

Mark Twain

priate if she chooses to lend it. What a daughter-in-law perceives as essential, a mother-in-law might perceive as frivolous.

Furthermore, even if the mother-in-law has ample resources, she cannot be expected to rescue her child from every unpleasant situation. This enables the child and does not provide for growth or maturation. A couple should not start their marriage indebted to the mother-in-law, as resentment is likely to flourish. This resentment might keep the mother-in-law and daughter-in-law's relationship at a distance.

Another hazard of lending money is the real or imagined debt placed on the married couple. A mother-in-law might make more demands on the young couple because she has confidence in the fact that they owe her, but she must not expect her son and daughter-in-law to viably become her domestics because they owe her money. A daughter-in-law may perceive any request from her mother-in-law as a probable compulsion, even if that is not the mother-in-law's intention.

"Education is an admirable thing, but it is well to remember from time to time that nothing that is worth knowing can be taught."

Oscar Wilde

Borrowing money creates land mines for all those concerned. It is therefore advisable to borrow only in dire need and when all other options have been considered. Give gifts from your heart and treasure any gift you receive. Never equate money with love. Money can foster jealousy, envy, and waste. Money has the potential to create a desire for things that we do not need or that we can do without, and it can make us self-indulgent and selfish. Although money is essential to life, it will never be an answer to problems.

1st Vignette

Ava was privileged to have enough money to splurge whenever she fancied. If her son Matt and his wife, Jill, needed any money, Ava was agreeable to give it to them.

> "Happiness is like a butterfly. The more you chase it, the more it will elude you. But if you turn your attention to other things, it comes and softly sits on your shoulder."
>
> Nathaniel Hawthorne

This appeared to be an ideal situation, but that, of course, was not the case. Ava indulged her grandchildren with gifts of toys and clothing on every birthday and holiday. Ava was pleased to be able to do this, but she was continually disappointed with Jill's reaction. Ava never flaunted her wealth, and she never demanded anything in return. Ava didn't understand Jill's attitude. Ava wasn't forcing Matt and Jill to take any money from her. Ava simply made it known that she was there to help them if they required assistance.

Ava recalled her grandson Mark's birthday. Ava had bought Mark more presents than she could count. Ava always took such delight in the children's reaction to

> "Never lose a chance of saying a kind word."
>
> William Makepeace Thackeray
> British writer

their gifts. Ava's father died when she was young, so Ava had grown up poor. Pleasing her grandchildren allowed Ava the pleasure of reliving her childhood the way she would have wanted, through her grandchildren.

Ava arrived at Matt and Jill's house loaded down with presents. Jill's mother, Jane, greeted Ava with a curt smile. Ava brushed past Jane and deposited her gifts on the kitchen table.

Mark squealed when he saw Ava and all of the presents. Ava immediately sat down at the kitchen table to enjoy a cup of coffee with Jane, who was visiting from out of town. Jane had little to say to Ava and quickly maneuvered herself into another room away from Ava.

The children, Mark and Lori, opened the gifts from Ava and squealed with delight. Jill encouraged them to open the gifts from their other grandmother. Whenever Mark opened a gift from Jane, there were explosions of delight from Jill to the many beautiful books her mother had given to the children. Jill told Mark and Lori that she would read some of the new books that night before

> "Riches and power are but gifts of blind fate, whereas goodness is the result of one's own merits."
>
> Heloise

bedtime. Jill thanked her mother for the gifts. Jill never thanked Ava, nor mentioned Ava's many gifts. Ava was deeply wounded.

Ava left Jill's house early and went home. Ava tried to make excuses for Jill and her mother, Jane. Ava knew that Jane was not wealthy, but maybe it was Jane's problem, and not Ava's, that it always ended up in a confrontation. Perhaps Jane was the one threatened by the gifts. Ava contemplated Jane's reaction, surmising that she was the one who equated the gifts to money. She came to the conclusion that Jane had the issue, not her. Jill's mother could not afford expensive gifts, and her childhood was as frugal as Ava's childhood had been. Still, Ava was wounded by Jill's reaction to the presents. The only people she pleased were the children. Ava smiled when she realized this fact because that was what it was all about anyway, and she didn't really care about assuming adults. Ava didn't have a semblance of hope at trying to comprehend Jill's attitude, but, at the moment, she was low on sympathy. Ava had been insulted so many times, and it was difficult for her to feel any kindness toward Jill at the moment. All Ava could think about was the fact that she'd grown up poor herself. She kept trying to tell herself

> *"Make a memory with your children, spend some time to show you care; toys and trinkets can't replace those precious moments that you share."*
>
> *Elaine Hardt*

to get over Jane and Jill's reaction and move past it.

Ava confided some of her feelings to her son, Matt. That night, Matt confronted Jill about the way she had treated his mother. Matt was tense, alert, and angry. Jill admitted that she was always overwhelmed with Ava's abundance of gifts. Jill stated that she appreciated Ava's gifts, but she never knew how to thank her in front of her own mother. Jill also admitted that she was very uncomfortable with the amount of gifts Ava lavished on the children. Matt wasn't listening. He slammed the door and went for a walk. Jill glanced across the room and saw Lori and Mark busily playing with the new toys from Ava. Jill sat down on the edge of the bed and cried.

> "Out of respect for things I was never destined to do, I have learned that my strengths are a result of my weaknesses, my success is due to my failures, and my style is directly related to my limitations."
>
> Billy Joel

1st Discussion

Money creates happiness and unhappiness. Ava spends money lavishly. She had little money growing up, so now it means nothing more to her than to spend it or give it away. Jill doesn't grasp the little meaning and value that Ava places on her money. Jill sees Ava's money as boasting and is confused with Ava's spending because Ava is not seeking thanks or rewards for herself. Jill cannot comprehend Ava's motives, but she believes Ava has motives. Ava, however, should not be offended because of her wealth. It ap-

> "All are architects of fate, so look not mournfully into the past. It comes not back again."
>
> Unknown

pears that Jill has to work on respecting Ava for who she is. Ava seems to be innocent of seeking to deliberately annoy anyone with her offerings. Ava enjoys sharing her possessions with her grandchildren and is not flaunting her wealth. Jill must acknowledge Ava's wealth and tolerate it and Ava's ability and desire to share it. If Ava's wealth is problematic for Jill, then she needs to rethink her own self-worth and possible feelings of inferiority that Ava's wealth appears to be fostering.

Perhaps the confusion for Jill has more to do with the seeds of doubt Jane has planted. Jill is probably more troubled about her mother's reaction to Ava's gifts than she is bothered by them herself. Jill is trying to protect her mother from the boastfulness of Ava's gifts. While Jill doesn't dislike Ava and is not really jealous of her, she is genuinely confused with all that Ava gives. Jill is wavering between her mother and Matt's mother. Jill's mother has complained to Jill about the abundance of gifts from Ava, and Jill considers it necessary to justify her mother's viewpoints. Jill is grateful to Ava, but can't show her appreciation outright because it would feel like a disloyalty to her own mother. Now Jill has been con-

> "Join the great company of those who make the barren places of life fruitful with kindness."
>
> Helen Keller

> "Remember that time is money. "
>
> Ben Franklin

fronted by Matt's same necessity of justifying his mother's feelings. This is a new circumstance and Jill is not sure how to handle the situation.

Jane is behaving rudely to Ava, and this is another obstruction that Jill needs to deal with if she truly wants a workable and respectable relationship with her mother-in-law. Ava is caught in the middle of Jill and her mother, and it seems Jill and Ava need to have the space to communicate. It would be practical for them to come to an understanding about the money and gifts. Ava could dispense of her many gifts to the children throughout the year, alleviating the huge pile of gifts given at one time. Ava's gifts could also be opened privately after Jill's mother returns home so that sensitivities wouldn't be an issue. This would protect her mother from the embarrassment of contrasting gifts. Jill and Ava have a lot to work through. If they can have a heart-to-heart discussion regarding the issues, it might be possible for them to reach a compromise.

> "The difference between the impossible and the possible lies in a person's determination."
>
> Tommy Lasorda

It's essential the children be taught that the gift of time is a very significant gift. Being so excited to receive their grandmother's gifts; they do not appreciate the true meaning of gift-giving. It is reasonable to assume that when the children

> *"And the trouble is if you don't risk anything, you risk even more."*
>
> *Erica Jona*

mature, they will assign more emphasis on the human quality of the relationship rather than the monetary value. If money is not equated with love, then Jill's mother should not feel degraded or threatened because of what she cannot afford. Jane needs to also bear in mind that she is buying gifts from her heart, and children do not know the cost of presents. When children are younger, they simply love presents. They do not understand why one grandparent may be able to give them more. This is a dilemma for the parents to solve. Sometimes an inexpensive, thoughtful gift is cherished more than an extremely pricey gift.

The children will quite viably move toward an appreciation and love for their grandparents, provided they have opportunities to share precious moments together. Likely, they will not equate their grandparents' love with the size or quantity of gifts. These concepts will not be understood immediately, but with time, they will be comprehended and the children will be the nobler for it and for having acquired the lesson.

> *"Every accomplishment large and small begins with the same decision: I'll try."*
>
> *Ted Key*

2nd Vignette

Brian and Amy were tired of paying exorbitant rent. They just couldn't seem to get ahead. Whenever they had a little bit of money saved up in their joint bank account, something in the house would need to be repaired. This ultimately forced them to take the money out of the bank and spend it. Amy wanted to buy a house. Brian also wanted a house, but he was nervous about taking all of their money out of the bank for this venture. Brian worried about unexpected problems. Brian liked to keep extra cash handy in case of an emergency.

After many discussions, they decided to ask Ann, Brian's mother, for a loan. Ann agreed immediately to give the couple five thousand dollars to complete what they considered necessary for a down payment on a house.

> "Fortune is a great deceiver. She sells very dear the things she seems to give us."
>
> Vincent Voiture

As the weeks passed, problems arose. Whenever Ann called for even the smallest matter, as she had always done in the past, Brian would rush over to take care of it. Ann would mention that it was not terribly important, but Brian would still drop everything instantly when Ann called.

Ann was surprised at Brian's immediate response, but she did not comprehend the reason behind it. Other incidents began to make Ann curious. Ann was surprised when Amy stopped dropping over for visits. Whenever Ann did see Amy, the conversations were curt and formal. Ann questioned Brian to no avail.

One day, Brian arrived at his mother's to fix a problem she was having with her car. Amy came with Brian and paced around the kitchen. Amy finally plunged into a chair, stomping her feet as she outstretched them. Ann questioned Amy's strange behavior and discovered that she and Brian had been on their way to a movie. Ann was upset and confused. Ann couldn't figure out why they hadn't just told her that they had plans. Ann cowered into her armchair. Amy relented when she saw her mother-in-law's frail, quivering frame. Amy sighed as the tears rolled down her cheeks as well. Ann apologized in a broken voice for the couple's ruined plans.

Brian entered the room and tightened his face as he looked at the two women. Brian broke the silence. "I owe you, Mom," he said. Ann was shocked and saddened. She had not meant for her gift to place such restrictions on Amy and Brian. All three had a lot of factors to discuss.

> "We make a living by what we get. But we make a life by what we give. "
>
> Sir Winston Churchill

2nd Discussion

After Ann, Amy, and Brian reflected on the situation, they sat down together and communicated their various considerations. Ann admitted being surprised and shaken when she realized that Amy and Brian felt guilty and indebted to her because of the borrowed money. Ann should have made it clear that she was not expecting them to cater to her every whim. She did not want them to become obligated to her in any way. Ann explained to her son and daughter-in-law that she was telling Brian what had to be done as she had always done before. She was not in any way suggesting that Brian do the jobs immediately.

Ann had not meant to drive a wedge between her son and daughter-in-law or in her relationship with them. Amy felt relieved to discover that Ann was not pressuring Brian to do more projects. Amy was sorry that she had wrongly concluded Ann's motives.

It is not always wise to borrow money from one's parents. If a couple chooses to borrow money, then a payment schedule should be set up immediately. All parties should agree to the conditions, and there should be no unstated requisites.

> "What is it in us that seeks the truth? Is it our minds or is it our hearts?"
>
> A Time To Kill

Brian had falsely assumed whenever his mother had a request, he had to jump and do it right away. Brian put this pressure on himself. Brian forgot that his mother chose to lend him the money. She did not put any demands to the agreement. Brian suffered from anxiety and a guilty conscience over the situation, which made him respond promptly. Brian should not have pressured himself.

Amy made her own assumptions because Brian had become uncommunicative. She concluded that Ann was pressuring Brian to do the many jobs. Amy blamed Ann and began resenting her. Ann and Amy had a good relationship before the borrowed money. Amy should have voiced her complaints to Ann. Amy had so much harbored anger that she lashed out at Ann and caused everything to erupt, which actually turned out to be a good thing. Ann, in her innocence, tried to help Amy and Brian. Ann should have paid better attention to Brian's unusually fast response time. She might have discovered his guilt and the burdensome pressure it placed on his shoulders. Ann was so happy to have things done swiftly that she did not consider Amy, who was waiting patiently at home. Ann really should have been more aware of Brian and Amy and their growing resentment. Their tense emotions were apparent at the surface and easy to recognize. This family is to be commended for confronting their problems and affecting a positive outcome.

> "The marvelous richness of human experience would lose something of rewarding joy, if there were not limitations to overcome. The hilltop hour would not be half so wonderful if there were no dark valleys to traverse."
>
> Helen Keller

Brian and Amy took control of their lives again and set up a payment schedule. They aspired to pay back the money they owed to Ann as soon as they could.

They did not want Ann to think they were doing things for her out of the guilt of owing her. Amy and Brian loved Ann and sought to assist her whenever they could. Both households began functioning smoothly again.

Reflections for Daughters-in-Law

Remember the potential emotional cost if you borrow money from your mother-in-law.

Expect to repay any money that you have borrowed from your mother-in-law.

Live within your means instead of wishing for material items you cannot afford. You will be a happier person.

Appreciate money given to you by your mother-in-law when there are no obligations expected, but appreciate the time she gives to you more.

Respect your mother-in-law's right to do what she pleases with her money. She can donate it, spend it, or throw it away. She does not have to give it to you, nor does she owe you an explanation.

Do not compare your mother's gifts to your mother-in-law's gifts. You cannot put prices on love.

Tolerate any gifts from your mother-in-law with graciousness. Your mother-in-law is different from you, and her gifts to you might be a reflection of her likes.

Consider any time your mother-in-law gives to you

as precious as a gift of money. It is actually worth more.

Keep your distance when there is a money problem between your husband and mother-in-law.

Reflections for Mothers-in-Law

Keep your gift-giving sincere so that you are not giving as a means to an end.

Allow your son and daughter-in-law time to repay any money they have borrowed, without a constant reminder.

Consider any time your daughter-in-law gives to you as precious as a gift of money. It is actually worth more.

Unconditionally accept your daughter-in-law's right to do what she wants with any gift she receives from you. It belongs to her, and she can toss it away if she chooses.

Allow your daughter-in-law to exhibit her own likes and dislikes.

Do not use your wealth to control or subdue your daughter-in-law.

Money should never be used to boast, brag, or belittle others.

Never allow your grandchildren to equate your money with your love for them.

Tolerate any gifts from your daughter-in-law with graciousness. Your daughter-in-law is different from you, and her gifts to you might be a reflection of her likes.

When you give expensive gifts, do not attach any obligations. Gifts should be given without restrictions.

Questions for Daughters-in-Law

1. Do your mother-in-law's gifts seem to be thoughtless?

   Always   Sometimes   Seldom

2. Do you like your mother-in-law's gifts more when you know the cost?

   Always   Sometimes   Seldom

3. Do you believe that your mother-in-law should share some of her wealth so that you and your husband can get a start on life?

   Always   Sometimes   Seldom

4. Have you ever questioned your mother-in-law's appreciation for gifts and money you have given to her?

   Always   Sometimes   Seldom

Questions for Mothers-in-Law

1. Do your daughter-in-law's gifts appear to be thoughtless?

   Always   Sometimes   Seldom

2. Do you like your daughter-in-law's gifts more when you know the cost?

   Always   Sometimes   Seldom

3. Do you put pressure on your son and daughter-in-law to help you out because you gave them a large monetary gift?

   Always   Sometimes   Seldom

4. Have you ever questioned your daughter-in-law's appreciation for gifts and money you have given to her?

   Always   Sometimes   Seldom

Money

5 JEALOUSY

Jealousy manifests itself in numerous manners. It appears in an endless range of circumstances. A daughter-in-law can be jealous of the attention her mother-in-law gives to her husband, another daughter-in-law, or the mother-in-law's own daughter. A daughter-in-law may dislike her husband's attention to his mother.

> "It is never too late to be what we might have been."
>
> George Elliot

A mother-in-law may feel animosity toward her daughter-in-law because of the attention her son gives to his wife. A mother-in-law may dislike how much attention her daughter-in-law bestows to her own mother.

The daughter-in-law's mother might resent any close relationship her daughter has with her mother-in-law. The list of the countless circumstances in which jealousy may manifest itself is indeed infinite.

Jealousy often arises when there are grandchildren. A mother-in-law may feel she does not have the same kind of access to the children that her daughter-in-law's mother has, or a mother-in-law may appear to favor her daughter's children over her son's children. It doesn't matter if this is fact or fiction if the daughter-in-law and mother-in-law perceive these fixations as a reality. Recognizing jealousy is one aspect, but surmounting the emotional confusion of jealousy is no minor accomplishment.

Son Praises Mother

If we are jealous, we cannot be ourselves. Most often, we sabotage our individual merit. Our husbands and sons cannot be themselves because they are staying closely monitored. Husbands are potentially resented by their wives if they praise their mothers and vice versa. Harmony is nonexistent in these situations.

Getting beyond the jealousy

> "In marriage, with children, at work, in any association-an ounce of praise of sincere appreciation of some act or attribute, can very often do more than a ton of fault finding. If we look for it, we can usually find in even the most unlikely, unlikable and incapable person, something to commend and encourage. Doubtless, it is a human frailty. But most of us, in the glow of feeling we have pleased, want to do more to please and knowing we have done well, want to do better."

and recognizing each woman's significance is worth the time and effort. Research shows that most sons have developed a playful attitude with their mothers as a carryover from childhood. In watching the interaction, it is easy to observe the loving lightheartedness between a mother and her son. When exploring this relationship through a daughter-in-law's eyes, a type of rivalry becomes apparent.

The mother-in-law is, quite understandably, the "other woman." A son who compliments his mother's cooking may encounter scornful, glaring eyes. One might ask what the son learns from this interaction. It is possible he learns to forget complimenting his mother if he wants peace with his wife. Certainly, there are some wives who might save their response of the episode for the car ride home. Perhaps, in these cases, at the time, the treatment of the situation may appear to be lighthearted, but it still remains caustic, as the dinner and the mother-in-law are derided in the car while traveling home.

> *"Before we can forgive one another we must understand one another."*
>
> *Anonymous*

At this moment, new mothers-in-law are at their most vulnerable period. They are unaware of the impact the bonds with their sons have on their new daughters-in-law. Acknowledging the tremendous effect their mothers-in-law had on their husbands is a crucial affirmation of acceptance for daughters-in-law,

"Whenever you are in conflict with someone, there is one factor that can make the difference between damaging your relationship and deepening it. That factor is attitude".

William James

who might find life more tranquil if they treaded lightly and bestowed smaller amounts of critique, if any at all, with regard to their mothers-in-law.

In general, most people love their mothers regardless of her faults. Consider the fact that we do not normally criticize our friends' mothers, yet we may be liberally scattering negative comments about our husbands' mothers. At this point, we must ask ourselves why. Do we feel inferior or fragile in the presence of our mother-in-law? Does she intimidate us? These are important questions to be mulled over.

Mothers nurture their children through the ordeals of physical and emotional illness. Constant reproaches or disapprovals of anyone's mother would realistically drive a wedge into a friendship of any kind. The love a husband and wife have for each other is stronger, but it will not withstand a barrage of insults lodged against one's mother. The daughter-in-law who cannot reserve her remarks may find that she has created an extremely painful situation for all those concerned. The marriage may well have been jeopardized.

"It is not for what we do that we are held responsible, but also for what we do not do."

Moliere

A mother-in-law might inadvertently upset her daughter-in-law by volunteering to come to her son's aid, and upon inquiry, she might discover that her daughter-in-law doesn't want her interfering. This could be as simple an occurrence as getting her son a cup of coffee or changing his baby for him when it's his turn to do it. As there are fewer occasions for the mother to be able to help her son, she most likely leaps at the chance to provide assistance when an occasion arises, unaware of the likely consequences of her actions. The same daughter-in-law who does not like the help her mother-in-law gives to her husband will presumably readily accept help for herself from her own mother, creating a double standard. The husband is the unwilling pawn and the mother-in-law the unwilling player.

> *"Envy is a symptom of lack of appreciation of our own uniqueness and self-worth. Each of us has something to give that no one else has."*
>
> *Elizabeth O'Connor*

It is not credible that a man places his mother before his wife, yet each woman can hold a special place in his heart. It is important to realize that your husband is a part of your mother-in-law. Perhaps we are creating a problem in the relationship from the beginning of a marriage when we display feelings of anger, hostility, chaos and, turmoil. A daughter-in-law must be confident about her place in the scheme of things. A daughter-in-law is most important and need not lack

> "Speak when you're angry, and you'll make the best speech you'll ever regret."
>
> Lawrence J. Peter

confidence.

Son Praises Wife

Mothers-in-law are obliged to remember to refrain from appraising their daughters-in-law. A mother-in-law may destroy her daughter-in-law, who is a worthy component in her son's life. This woman is the one your son selected as the recipient of his true love. She is or possibly will be the mother of his children. Perpetual disapproval will thrust them away from you because of the emotional suffering. Your son will always love you, but he will not be capable of withstanding the persistent assault on the woman who is his wife. Support your daughter-in-law with statements of admiration. Make it a high priority to use discretion.

Keep in mind that active aggression is erroneous, but being passively aggressive is also a mistake. It is best to refrain from discussing your son's former girlfriends. This could be a deliberate act of passive aggression if you are unable to curb this discussion. Even if you are not ostensibly praising earlier girlfriends, mentioning them in conversation to offend your son's wife is purposely instigating issuances for your son and daughter-in-law.

> "It's what you learn after you know it all that counts. "
>
> John Wooden

In our hearts, we are aware that all of us have failings and these girls from your son's past are no exception. They were just as imperfect as the woman he married. They are just as imperfect as all of us. They may only appear to have been wonderful because they did not become your daughter-in-law.

A mother-in-law may be envious of the attention her son gives to his wife. The reasons for this jealousy are innumerable. It is not up to the daughter-in-law to try to fathom her mother-in-law's jealousy, only to recognize and accept it. Jealousy thrives everywhere and nobody is immune. Lack of attention drives anyone to jealousy.

We do not walk in another's shoes. We do not recognize the hardships or agony or pain that they have had to endure. Thus, many of us may be jealous of factors that are not even real. Sometimes we think we have knowledge of what the situation is, but we could be quite mistaken. The wonderful things we notice on the exterior of a person might be purely surface facade. It is likely the pain, anguish, and worry another person deals with is hidden from view.

> "Men soon the faults of others learn a few their virtues too, find out, but is there one I have a doubt who can his own defects discern?"
>
> Sanskrit Proverb

If we were permitted to switch places with another per-

111

son, we probably would not aspire to be that person for any lengthy amount of time. We credibly might be very gratified to get back to our own life and our own problems. We surely must never assume that factors are as they appear.

Mothers-in-law should refrain from comparing their children. Research tells us of sibling rivalry. This rivalry may be enhanced if a mother-in-law elects to compare grandchildren or adult children's jobs or homes. These comparisons degrade your children and yourself. What each child accomplishes is worthy of admiration. All children deserve our love and attention. All are special and unique with their own qualities, which will manifest in time. We all, for the most part, have a lifetime to promote our qualities. Some of us may not get started as early as the rest of us, and some of us stray from the usual path, but still offer our own unique accomplishments.

> "He who will not reflect is a ruined man."
>
> Asian Proverb

A mother-in-law should try to see beyond the visible, taking the whole person into account, and refuse to pass judgment. What another accomplishes and values is subjective. What each of us chooses in life is also subjective. A mother-in-law must respect the choices her children make and permit them to control their own lives. A mother-in-law can carry this further and attempt to perceive the special attributes of her daughter-in-law and not dismiss her for the qualities that are possibly absent. This is also true for the daughter-in-law, who must attempt to witness her mother-in-laws virtues.

Likewise, a daughter-in-law should give her mother-in-law the benefit of the doubt. The selections your mother-in-law made were produced in respectable conviction, given the circumstances and situation at the time. You cannot imagine or understand that actual phase in your mother-in-law's life. It is easy to use retrospection and state publicly that she made poor decisions. If you try to understand and accept your mother-in-law's selections, it will allow you to be liberated in your own medleys.

"To find a fault is easy; to do better may be difficult."

Plutarch

It is believable that when we consider ourselves to be inferior, we do not set high goals for ourselves. This is an injustice to us. We should not set goals that are impossible for us to attain, but we should be wary of permitting others to set our goals. Ambitions are personal and need to be redefined and revised regularly. We should always attempt to have and accomplish our objectives. Trying to live up to another's aims for us is impractical. It realizably should be compulsory for us to make and live up to our own aspirations. If we choose to make major decisions that hurt and belittle another, then we must be aware of the consequences of our actions. A trace of jealousy may always be present, but it can be kept in restraint. All of us struggle to balance our lives with peace and happiness. We can presume on the surface that others have life easier than we do, but everyone struggles. Some hide the labor better than others, and some complain less, but the grind is enduring for all. Supporting each other as well as managing the jealous tendencies can make life so much easier.

The Daughter-in-law's Mother

The mother of the daughter-in-law should not be left out of the mix. She can hold the recipe for success or failure in the relationship her daughter has with her mother-in-law. Mothers sometimes influence their daughters against becoming too close with their mothers-in-law because of their own insecurities. They feel threatened by any positive relationship their daughter could feasibly have with her mother-in-law. They might influence and insist that their daughter keep her mother-in-law detached from any genuine emotional closeness.

> "Is there one word which may serve as a rule of practice for all one's life? The Master said is not Reciprocity such a word? What you do not want done to yourself, do not do to others."
>
> Confucius

It is reasonable to assume that a daughter-in-law could possibly enjoy her mother-in-law's company, but feels a twinge of betrayal of her own mother if she allows her mother-in-law to become too intimate. Mixed feelings consume the daughter-in-law, but if she can work through this predicament, there is a possibility of a strong alliance between herself and her mother-in-law.

It appears that some daughters-in-law find it difficult or unviable to crawl out from their mother's grasp and take charge of their own lives and opinions. The result is the loss of a potentially satisfying relationship with their mothers-in-law. All parents have within their power the ability to instill self-reproach in their adult children. In our many relationships, the mother-in-law and daughter-in-law relationship is no exception. What should be reflected upon is the potential for all to be happy if an agreement to live and let live is practiced. Certainly, there is room for all bonds of affection. It is not only important for the mothers of boys to let their sons go so that they can fly to great heights, but also for the mothers of daughters to also let go and allow their daughters to do the same.

> "Envy is a littleness of soul, which cannot see beyond a certain point, and if it does not occupy the whole space, feels itself excluded."
>
> Wm. Hazlitt
> characteristics
> 1823

1st Vignette

Helen was exhausted from babysitting her three grandchildren. Her eldest son, Jim, was trying to get a carpentry business going. There wasn't a lot of money, so Jim depended on the extra money his wife's paycheck brought in. To save money, Jim asked his mother, Helen, to babysit temporally. The children were young, but Jim and Norma had no choice. Jim believed that it was going to be temporary. It was extremely important that Norma keep her job because they were also depending on her medical insurance. The baby was constantly plagued with an ear infection, which was a constant reminder of their need for medical insurance. The fundamental truth was, they both needed to be working.

The children were one, three, and four. The babysitting proved difficult, but manageable for Helen. Jim had promised her that as soon as a good job came along, he would take it. Helen never questioned what Jim's idea of a good job was. Jim said when he got a good job, Norma would quit her job and stay home with the children until they were of school age. That was the original plan three years ago. Currently, Helen was still babysitting. Norma received a promotion and loved her job.

> "Many men owe the grandeur of their lives to their tremendous difficulties."
>
> Haddon Spurgeon

Helen was coping, when her second son, John, approached her with a request. John asked Helen if she would babysit for his six-month-old daughter. His wife, Lisa, stood at his side and waited for Helen's reply. Helen hesitated. Lisa retorted how Helen was in such a routine with Norma's children that one more shouldn't make a difference. Helen had no choice but to reply in the affirmative. If she had babysat for Jim for three years already, how could she say no to John? Helen agreed, and six months later, the baby was getting too difficult for her to manage.

The baby was poking at everything. Helen was exhausted and upset. Helen saw no signs of Jim taking another job, and since Norma's promotion, there were no signs of Norma quitting, either. John and Lisa were busy with their jobs, and Helen was full of her own sad thoughts.

1st Discussion

> "Character builds slowly but it can be torn down with incredible swiftness."
>
> Faith Baldwin

It is important to have all of the facts when we agree to any long-term arrangements. This story proves that point. There was no time limit to these babysitting arrangements. Helen was given no real tangible end to the job. Helen was rendered to sense guilt if she didn't help Jim and Norma. They needed the insurance Norma's job provided. Lisa and John were jealous of the arrangement that Norma and Jim had. After all, they reasoned Norma and Jim were paying very little for excellent child care. We can see that jealousy abounds. The loser was Helen.

Neither daughter-in-law considered the welfare of her mother-in-law. They paid no attention to the strain it was causing Helen. Because Helen wanted to keep peace and not show favorites, she was caught in the middle of a jealousy struggle. Neither daughter-in-law should have made Helen responsible for her money problems. As sad for them as Helen felt, she should not have taken on the responsibility without a termination date. Both daughters-in-law were competing for their mother-in-law's time, attention, and services. Both couples played on Helen's conscience. Guilt should never play a role in making a decision.

2nd Vignette

> "Life has taught me that it is not for our faults that we are disliked and even hated, but for our qualities."
>
> Bernard Berenson

Deb was so happy for her son, Pete, and his wife, Megan. They had their second child days before. Their oldest child was a daughter. She was now two and quite a handful. Deb was a major asset to Megan. She helped with the babysitting throughout the pregnancy. Deb was always willing to give Megan a break. She also had them over for dinner often or sent meals over to them.

It was great having her son and daughter-in-law living close by. It allowed her the opportunity to lend a hand with things. Megan's parents lived out of state. After the baby was born, they came to visit with Megan. One day, Deb stopped by to visit Megan and the new baby, which Deb had not yet held. Donna, who was Megan's mother, was holding and rocking the baby. Deb took a seat and silently waited her turn to hold the baby. Donna made no effort to give her the baby. Megan was busy and paid no attention to her mother or mother-in-law.

Two hours past, and Deb was anxious to get home. She had still not held the baby. Megan reached for her sleeping baby. Deb asked if she could hold her sleeping granddaughter. Megan replied that the baby was tired and she was going to put her in for a nap. The rebuff was like a slap in the face for Deb. She rose to leave, unable to face Donna or Megan. She was consequently dejected as she made her way home.

Deb complained to her son. Her son replied that he assumed she enjoyed doing things for them. He stated that he did not know that he was inconveniencing her as Deb implied. Deb was even more frustrated. She had not meant to sound like a whining person. Deb really did enjoy doing things for her son and daughter-in-law, but now her son thought she didn't. Deb was feeling worse by the minute. She regretted having spoken at all and just couldn't find the correct words to remedy the situation she found herself in. Deb did not feel appreciated; she felt used.

2nd Discussion

Donna was probably aware of the fact that her time with the baby was limited. She made no effort to allow Deb to hold the baby because she knew Deb would have many chances. Megan was so proud of her new daughter and so happy to have her mother visiting that she basically ignored her mother-in-law.

Deb was jealous of Megan's mother, Donna. Deb could have waited the few days, allowing Donna some quality time alone with her daughter. Deb likely could visit with Megan after Megan's mother had gone home. As hurtful as this situation was for Deb, it was a difficult one for Megan.

Megan was giving all of her attention to her own mother. We can appreciate the happiness that Megan was experiencing, but to ignore her mother-in-law, who had been a positive presence throughout her pregnancy, was inexcusable. Even if Deb had not been helpful during the pregnancy, she still deserved some attention and recognition as the other grandmother. Deb could have been patient and permitted Megan to visit with her mother alone.

It might have been wiser for Deb to give Megan some private time with her mother. This was of the essence, especially because Donna lived out of state. The baby, after all, would be around for a long time. There would be many other times to hold and rock the baby. Deb could, and should, have postponed her visit to her new grandchild for a later time. Megan surely might have given Deb a few moments to hold the baby prior to Deb's departure. This in no way would have hindered or taken time away from the mother-daughter visit.

Jealous misunderstandings abound. Donna is obviously jealous of Deb's ten-minute, close access to Megan and the baby. Living in another state places her farther away from the daily activities and accomplishments of the children. Deb is jealous of Megan's indulgence of her mother. Because Deb is willing to do the menial work, she believes this should somehow entitle her to special privileges. A show of gratitude might have controlled and alleviated the tension for all those affected. Megan shows inexperience at handling a difficult situation in a fair manner. Megan does not know how to deal with her mother or mother-in-law when given a sticky situation. She does nothing, which only intensifies things.

Reflections for Daughters-in-Law

Remember your mother-in-law is important to your husband. They are like a tapestry, interwoven forever. If you undo one, then you have undone the other.

Allow your husband's mother a position in the family. His roots began with her. She is a part of his history.

Refrain from wounding and demeaning your mother-in-law. A well-intentioned compliment will go a lot further.

Your mother-in-law has other concerns, cares, and love for her other children and daughters-in-law. Allow her the space to care for others.

Appreciate the fact that your mother-in-law is of a different generation and may have difficulty coping with the current attitudes and roles that men and women are exhibiting.

Competing with your mother-in-law creates a no-win situation. Being right or wrong is not as important as how well everyone's sense of worth remains intact.

Maintain your own sense of self-worth and live up to your own goals.

Nurture the love and closeness you have with your husband.

Appreciate your husband's attention and cherish it.

Offer praise to your mother-in-law. This will enhance your satisfaction and give you the respect of your husband.

Reflections for Mothers-in-Law

Treat your daughter-in-law in a similar way that you treat your own daughter or other daughters-in-law.

Remember that your daughter-in-law plays a significant role in your son's life.

Encourage your son and daughter-in-law to reach for their hopes and dreams. Be interested, or at the very least, act interested.

Remember that praise and gratefulness go a long way in healing pain, frustration, and envy.

Try to be above suspicion so that your daughter-in-law may trust and confide in you if she chooses.

Refrain from bringing up your son's past girlfriends. It does not enhance his image. It will erode his relationship with you as well as his new girlfriend or wife.

Praise all of your daughters-in-law and children. Building everyone's self-confidence enhances everyone's relationships.

Allow your son and daughter-in-law space to confide in each other.

Accept whatever visiting arrangements your son

and daughter-in-law make. If they are welcome and enjoy your company, they are sure to return more often.

Your daughter-in-law must be her own person and live up to her own goals. Support her efforts.

Questions for Daughters-in-Law

1. Do you compare the gifts your mother-in-law gives to you to the ones that your mother-in-law gives to her daughter?

   Always   Sometimes   Seldom

2. Does your mother-in-law question you about private matters?

   Always   Sometimes   Seldom

3. Do you expect your husband to shop for his own mother's gifts?

   Always   Sometimes   Seldom

4. Do you make your husband crazy with questions about his mother?

   Always   Sometimes   Seldom

5. Do you believe that your husband should never confide in his mother?

   Always   Sometimes   Seldom

6. Do you feel that your husband gives too much time and attention to his mother?

   Always   Sometimes   Seldom

Questions for Mothers-in-Law

1. Do you feel your daughter-in-law puts a lot more thought into the gifts she gives to her mother versus the gifts she gives to you?

   Always   Sometimes   Seldom

2. Do you ask your son and daughter-in-law many personal questions?

   Always   Sometimes   Seldom

3. Do you mention any occasions when you have seen your son's ex-girlfriend?

   Always   Sometimes   Seldom

4. Do you make your son crazy with questions about his wife?

   Always   Sometimes   Seldom

5. Do you think your son should tell you everything that he discusses with his wife?

   Always   Sometimes   Seldom

6. Do you believe your son pampers his wife too much?

   Always   Sometimes   Seldom

Mother-in-law Daughter-in-law Dilemma

6 RESPECT

Consideration should always be granted to another person. A mother-in-law's fairness to her daughter-in-law is out of respect for her son, and a daughter-in-law's fairness to her mother-in-law is out of respect for her husband.

> *"To know even one life has breathed easier because you have lived, this is to have succeeded."*
>
> *Ralph Waldo Emerson*

We need to saturate our hearts with appreciation, deliberation, and honor. Treating another person decently or compassionately is demonstrating regard. It is acceptable to give others respect, but it is necessary to first be aware of another's existence. There are times when we simply do not see others or their needs and desires. Becoming aware of other people and their wishes can plant the seeds for nurturing and respect. Many times we are not cognizant of the countless behaviors we exhibit that offend others. We hurt others by our actions or what we say. It requires practice to focus attention on others. Tuning into another's circumstance of the mind permits us to empathize with what they might be pondering or feeling.

A mother-in-law might be unaware that her daughter-in-law has been up all night with a crying baby. If a daughter-in-law shares this information with her mother-in-law, the mother-in-law can show consideration for and assist her daughter-in-law by taking charge of the baby so that her daughter-in-law can get some much needed rest. A mother-in-law can simply be a sounding board for her daughter-in-law's complaints. A mother-in-law can allow her daughter-in-law to defuse her frustration by simply listening to her concerns.

> "A life spent making mistakes is not only more honorable but more useful than a life spent doing nothing."
>
> George Bernard Shaw

A daughter-in-law should key into her mother-in-law's complaints. Her mother-in-law may not always feel well. A daughter-in-law might consider all of this before judging her mother-in-law's frame of mind.

Sometimes through common sense we demonstrate respect. Helping a daughter-in-law cope with her children is considerate. Helping a mother-in-law clear off a table is appreciative. The little things mothers-in-law and daughters-in-law do for each other creates the bonds of respect they have for each other. Showing respect is also necessary when discussing our dissimilar opinions.

We can reject our mother-in-law's concepts for decorating, spending money, or child rearing without rejecting her. We can never be too sure that our way is

"Darkness cannot drive out darkness; only light can do that. Hate cannot drive out hate; only love can do that."

Martin Luther King.

the better way for doing things just because it is the current thinking.

Mothers-in-law can reject their daughters-in-law's concepts for working, spending money, dressing, or taking care of the children without rejecting their daughters-in-law. Give your daughter-in-law credit for venturing into the unknown and attempting to apply a new concept. You may feel it necessary to wear lace to a wedding; your daughter-in-law may wear pants or a skirt. You cannot tell her how to dress.

Research shows there are complaints from daughters-in-law when mothers-in-law visit unexpectedly. Daughters-in-law prefer formal invitations. Some mothers-in-law complain that they never get invited to their daughter-in-law's house for dinner. If they do get invited, the meal is thrown together from a box. Other mothers-in-law stated that if they just dropped by unexpectedly, they got a cold shoulder. They did not feel welcome. Some mothers-in-law felt like intruders.

"Nobody as long as he moves about among the currents of life, is without trouble."

Carl Jung

The daughters-in-law complained that they worked a full-time job and had children to contend with. If they invited their mothers-in-law, they did not cook too much because they are not "gourmet cooks." Some

131

daughters-in-law stated that their mothers-in-law stopped by unexpectedly to spy on them and to catch them and their house in complete disarray. One daughter-in-law stated, "She just wants to check up on my house-cleaning habits and cooking ability."

> "While on a walk one day, I was surprised to see a man hoeing his garden while sitting in his chair. What laziness! I thought. But suddenly I saw leaning against his chair, a pair of crutches. The man was at work despite his handicap. The lessons I learned about snap judgments that day have stayed with me for years now. The crosses people bear are seldom in plain sight."
>
> Annette Ashe - Guideposts

The truth for both mothers-in-law and daughters-in-law lies someplace in the middle. If a mother-in-law or a daughter-in-law is trying to find imperfections, then they will easily find them without much effort. There are imperfections in the best of us, but also worthiness in the worst of us. Respect requires the ability to ignore another's shortcomings. If we display appreciation for another, we might be more considerate in our judgments and opinions. By being aware of another's struggles, we may connect on a higher level with that person and recognize his or her worth. Realizably, if we appreciate another's challenges, it may conceivably allow us to appreciate them.

> "A moment's insight is sometimes worth a life's experience."
>
> Oliver Wendell

The daughter-in-law should not be expected to produce a gourmet meal. Many mothers-in-law agreed that boxed pizza was just fine as long as they got an invitation to come over, as they felt the company was the best. Likewise, the daughters-in-law agreed that an unexpected visit now and again was okay, provided there was a refrain of criticism. Both factions wished for pleasant conversation.

1st Vignette

Sue, a mother-in-law for all of three years, was distraught because her daughter-in-law refused to buy furniture or curtains for her house. Sue also deemed her daughter-in-law's housecleaning effort poor. Her daughter-in-law, Monica, stated to Sue many times that she wanted to wait and buy what she wanted when she had the money. Monica also said that housecleaning was not a principal priority. She had more important things to do. Sue took this as an affront. Sue considered herself an excellent housekeeper. She took pride in her beautiful house and in her attempts to keep it neat and clean. The circumstances were distressing for both Monica and Sue. Each had a sense of deter-

> "If A is success in life, then A equals X plus Y plus Z. Work is X, Y is play and Z is keeping your mouth shut."
>
> Albert Einstein

> "We know what a person thinks not when he tells us what he thinks but by his actions."
>
> Isaac Bashevis

mination that was dissimilar from the others. Sue was insulted by Monica's attitude toward keeping a house. Sue believed it was a reflection of the care her son, Ben, might be receiving. In Monica's thinking, this could not be further from the truth. Monica understood that she wasn't performing mundane tasks that were unappealing. Monica also refused to clutter her house with items she did not like and could not relate to. She had no problem waiting to buy what she wanted. She and Ben would continue to sleep on the mattress on the floor until further notice. Sue could not believe this situation. She shook her head and dejectedly surrendered by refusing to approach the subject again. This was a relief to Monica who sensed she finally was allowed a little peace.

Monica and Ben did not have the money to purchase the more expensive furniture and curtains that they preferred. Monica refused to buy cheaper items merely to have curtains on the windows or chairs in the kitchen. Monica was willing to postpone her purchase until they could afford to buy the expensive items she craved.

> "You can tell more about a person by what he says about others than you can by what others say about him."
>
> Anonymous

Sue was distraught. Her own home was immaculate and orderly. Monica enjoyed living in

> "Love is strengthened by working through conflicts together."
>
> Anonymous

her home the way it was, which was disorganized and chaotic. Monica and Ben had no curtains on the windows, and their mattress was thrown on the floor. Pillows were scattered on the floor to be used as seats. Ben and Monica were content. They would wait for what they wanted despite Sue's prodding.

Sue's thoughts on the subject were entirely different. She believed that Monica should put a lot more time into her homemaking effort. At one point, Sue became very agitated. She viewed their home as a reflection of herself. This was a mistake. Sue was embarrassed for anyone in the family to visit Ben and Monica because of the craziness of their home.

One day, Sue decided to give Monica some discarded furniture and curtains. Sue also went to Monica's and cleaned the house from top to bottom. Sue believed that Monica would be so impressed that she would keep the house that way. Monica accepted the gifts and hung the curtains. After a month had passed, the dog had ripped the bottom of the curtains to shreds. The dog had also chewed on the arms of the chairs. When Sue stopped over for a visit, she could not believe her eyes. The house was in complete disarray. Sue was destroyed. Her relationship with

> "He who flings mud loses a lot of ground."
>
> Anonymous

her daughter-in-law deteriorated rapidly.

1st Discussion

The sad part of this story is that the mother-in-law and daughter-in-law did not intentionally aspire to hurt each other, but they did. The daughter-in-law did not respect her mother-in-law's gifts.

Monica might have appreciated her help with the cleaning, but she could not keep the house as neat and organized as Sue kept her house because she did not believe it a necessity. Monica never really fancied the service or the objects. She did not ask for them. Monica actually presumed that by taking Sue's gifts, she was initiating an atmosphere of ambiance for Sue.

> "Every day do something that will inch you closer to a better tomorrow."
>
> Doug Firebaugh

When Sue became upset with Monica, the anger and resentful Monica felt about the gifts exploded into a wrath. She was pleased the dog ate the items because she was relieved of something she never wanted in the first place. If Monica had thought about her mother-in-law's generosity, she might have contemplated before allowing the dog to destroy them. If Monica had considered her mother-in-law's state of mind, she might have taken better care of them. If Monica really did not want them and resented her mother-in-law's interference, then she should have refused the gifts.

Sue should not have forced her daughter-in-law to

take the gifts without her approval. Sue should have considered Monica's point of view on the matter. She ought to have respected her daughter-in-law's justification to have her own preferences. After Sue gave the gifts to Monica, Sue had no right to dictate how Monica should handle them. Monica had the right to handle the objects as she pleased. They were given to her as gifts, and it was her privilege to do with them as she wished. The gifts could technically be used or abused as Monica desired. Cleaning Monica's house was not going to convert Monica into a housecleaner.

> "Anxious hearts are very heavy, but a word of encouragement does wonders!"
>
> Proverbs 12:25

We all have our own priorities and need to respect everyone's right to have their own in the order they choose. Sue expected her daughter-in-law to feel guilty about the way the gifts were abused. Sue disregarded the fact that Monica had not wanted the gifts to begin with. When Sue forced her to take them, Monica relinquished and accepted them for her husband's sake. Monica believed the gifts to be used items and worthless, and that is the way she mistreated them. Monica was not arrogant; she simply did not appreciate them. Monica made it known that she placed little value on used gifts. Neither Sue nor Monica reflected on the other's motives. Both women only thought about their own point of view.

2nd Vignette

Cassie was an easy woman to talk to. She began her rendition of her mother-in-law, Nancy. Cassie had been married to Sean for over ten years. Cassie had a twinkle in her eyes every time Nancy's name was mentioned. Cassie recalled and retold a couple of funny and interesting stories. Her lush plants were obvious, and Cassie recalled one particular account about her plants and her mother-in-law. Cassie began her account with an amusing smile.

> "The mind is no match with the heart in persuasion; constitutionality is no match with compassion."
>
> Everett M. Dirkson

When Cassie and Sean had been married for about five years, they lived a short distance from Nancy. Cassie remembered how busy she was when her children were much younger than they were now. Cassie said how much she loved plants, but she admitted that, at times, she forgot to water them. Her mother-in-law was a green thumb plant person. When Nancy would stop by for a visit, she would pull out all of the brown, dead leaves and water Cassie's plants. Nancy would then instruct Cassie on how to take better care of them.

If Nancy came unexpectedly and Cassie had piles of laundry all over the kitchen floor, Nancy just stepped over them and made her way to a chair without blinking an eye or losing a step. Nancy never mentioned the dirty laundry. Cassie laughed. Nancy would invite Cassie to lunch. Nancy always chose the restaurant, but she allowed Cassie to have veto power. Cassie recalled using her veto power only once. Nancy had chosen a fish restaurant, and Cassie hated fish. That particular time they chose a restaurant they both agreed on.

Cassie always had three plants hanging in the den by the window, as she currently did. The plants were full of brown leaves and drooping green ones. Cassie mentioned her busy schedule. She drew attention to the three plants and recollected how they were looking about as attractive as they had the day her mother-in-law decided to come for an unexpected visit. Cassie continued with her story.

> "Never look down on anybody unless you're helping him up."
>
> The Reverend Jesse Jackson

Nancy had not been over for three weeks. She usually called Cassie the day before she planned on visiting. Cassie hung up the phone and studied her three sick plants and made her decision. Cassie was not in the mood for an instruction, so she marched to the garden shop and bought three plants just like her dying ones. The next day, Cassie hung up the plants, picked up the house, and waited for her mother-in-law to arrive.

When Nancy walked into the front room and spotted the fully green plants, she remarked how beautiful they were. Nancy then turned to her daughter-in-law and said, "You must have just bought them and replaced the other three."

Cassie was shocked. She stared at her mother-in-law, and then they both burst out laughing. For the rest of the visit, if either woman mentioned the plants, they had another laugh. Cassie spoke with love about Nancy. Cassie said how Nancy always went on vacation with them. Nancy would babysit while Cassie and Sean went out by themselves. The only drawback to having Nancy on vacation with them was that she had to sit in the front seat of the car with Sean. Nancy would get car sick if she didn't sit up front, although Cassie had never seen Nancy get carsick. Cassie chuckled. Her amusing stories are inspiring. They proved that the mother-in-law and daughter-in-law could manage a compatible relationship with honesty, understanding, respect, and a dose of humor.

> "It is not good for all your wishes to be fulfilled; through sickness; you recognize the value of health, through evil; the value of good; through a hunger; satisfaction; through exertion, the value of rest."
>
> From an old Greek book of wisdom

2nd Discussion

Cassie and Nancy clearly have a wonderful relationship. They enjoy each other's company. Cassie never felt the need to force her mother-in-law into the backseat of the car to prove or disprove her carsickness theory. Cassie accepted her mother-in-law's word and respected her mother-in-law.

> *"The bond that links your true family is not one of blood, but of respect and joy in each other's life."*
>
> *Richard Bach*

Nancy was respectful of Cassie as well. She never mentioned the laundry. Nancy pretended not to see the laundry. Nancy gave her son, Sean, and Cassie space and time. She blended in so as to become a part of their lives without intruding. She did not try to influence their actions. Nancy never attempted to dictate instructions. She did offer advice, which Cassie felt free to accept or reject. Cassie was not pressured by Nancy's advice.

Both women liked each other. They saw faults, but overlooked them. Both women dwelled on the good things about the other person, and this made their relationship stronger. They were not competing or comparing. They were decent and fair with each other. Most of all, they were respectful.

Cassie deferred to her mother-in-law at times, and Nancy deferred to her daughter-in-law. Cassie and Nancy's relationship would make many mothers-in-law and daughters-in-law envious, yet all of us are capable of such a relationship with a little work, effort, and respect.

> *"Peace cannot be kept by force. It can only be achieved by understanding."*
>
> *Albert Einstein*

Reflections for Daughters-in-Law

Tell your mother-in-law when you have been up with a sick baby or child. She cannot read your mind or sympathize with you if you do not tell her.

Give your mother-in-law space to show love, care, and concern for her son, your husband. Respect the fact that she is his mother.

Respect the time your mother-in-law gives to you through her invitations to dinner, babysitting, or simply cheering you up.

Honor your mother-in-law on Mother's Day. She has not stopped being a mother because her children are raised.

Remember to treat your mother-in-law the way you would want your daughter-in-law to treat you one day.

Do not accept things from your mother-in-law that you do not intend to take care of or use. Simply say no.

Help out with dishes and with meals at holidays and other times you are asked to dinner. Your mother-in-law should not be expected to do it all by herself.

Norms are subject to change. You may reject your mother-in-law's ideas without rejecting her.

You are not giving up power or control when you defer to your mother-in-law. You are only being appreciative of the fact that she is a human being worthy of respect.

Accept that no one is always right or wrong. All of us are a little bit right and a little bit wrong.

Reflections for Mothers-in-Law

Tell your daughter-in-law about your aches and pains. Putting on a smile when you are not feeling well will confuse your daughter-in-law. She cannot empathize with you if she does not know how you feel.

Remember when your daughter-in-law becomes a mother; she deserves attention and respect on Mother's Day. Be willing to share the day.

Show your daughter-in-law appreciation when your daughter-in-law defers to what you want or where you want to go.

Offer your items and your help, but never force them onto your daughter-in-law. You cannot expect her to treasure what you treasure.

Give your daughter-in-law the courtesy of a phone call before you show up at her front door.

Refrain from telling your daughter-in-law how to run her household or how to decorate it. Allow her to use her own sense and judgment.

Do not give so much advice that your daughter-in-law stops listening as soon as you begin to talk. Respect her techniques and stylishness.

Do not allow guilt to be a part of your repertoire.

Accept your daughter-in-law's simple meals. You have had many more years of experience, and norms and attitudes have changed. She may also be working full time with little time left over for preparing meals.

Do not expect your daughter-in-law to be happy to see you if you arrive unexpectedly at her doorstep without a phone call.

Questions for Mothers-in-Law

1. Do you compliment your daughter-in-law's style of clothing or the way she decorates her home?

    Always   Sometimes   Seldom

2. Do you ever overlook anything negative about your daughter-in-law?

    Always   Sometimes   Seldom

3. Do you give your daughter-in-law allowances and excuses when her house is messy?

    Always   Sometimes   Seldom

4. Do you ever allow your daughter-in-law to get the last word in when you are discussing something?

    Always   Sometimes   Seldom

5. Do you keep personal things about your daughter-in-law private?

    Always   Sometimes   Seldom

Questions for Daughters-in-Law

1. Do you joke about the way your mother-in-law does things and her old-fashioned ideas?

   Always   Sometimes   Seldom

2. Do you consistently get the last word in when you have a discussion with your mother-in-law?

   Always   Sometimes   Seldom

3. Do you constantly see your mother-in-law's faults?

   Always   Sometimes   Seldom

4. Do you discuss personal things about your mother-in-law with others?

   Always   Sometimes   Seldom

5. Do you forget your mother-in-law is older and may not be as capable?

   Always   Sometimes   Seldom

7 CONFIDENCE

Developing your self-worth enhances your self-esteem. We are as diverse as we are similar. Individuals are unique in their numerous talents and abilities. Accepting our individuality with graciousness allows diversity to govern our lives in harmony. A daughter-in-law or mother-in-law should refrain from questioning every word or action the other verbalizes or executes. When interpreting another's behaviors or expressions, there is a multitude of interpretations. Our minds may wreak havoc on our emotions, and the truth might conceivably get lost.

> "You gain strength courage and confidence by every experience in which you really stop to look fear in the face."
>
> Eleanor Roosevelt

Self-Doubt

Confidence is important to our survival. If we have faith in our own knowledge, we are less likely to allow the daily defeats and snubs to affect our ability and dignity.

In practicality, the lives of others do not necessarily

revolve around our life. We cannot assume people are focusing attention on us. When we distort what is said and done, misinterpretations are made.

Doubting ourselves causes us to be less humble. Sensitivity will account for concealment and embarrassment. This can make us act pretentious. Our frail egos analyze mistakes. Hiding from faults portrays a false image. Being insecure engenders a desire to be exact and be paid attention to. A mother-in-law or daughter-in-law is obliged to prove she is capable. Failure threatens our self-esteem.

> *"Life is no brief candle to me. It is a sort of splendid torch which I have got hold of for the moment, and I want to make it burn as brightly as possible before handing it on to future generations."*
>
> *George Bernard Shaw*

When our performance is inadequate, we are anxious about the harsh judgment of others, potentially our mother-in-law or daughter-in-law, and this leads us to self-doubt.

We may perceive ourselves as inferior, yet we yearn to emerge outstanding. All of this doubt and anxiety leads to control, which may highlight a person's life. We may be comfortable if we make the rules, know the rules, and execute the plan. This ensures fewer errors, which are abhorred. We reasonably feel self-assured when we may express and carry

> *"He knows the water best who has waded through it."*
>
> *Danish Proverb*

149

> "No one is ever beaten unless he gives up the fight"
>
> W. Beran Wolfe

out all that we desire. Even when we lack the support of others, it is relevant we support ourselves.

Regretting our words and actions potentially generates turmoil, which reasonably spawns doubt in the way others perceive our ability to handle matters. When we demonstrate confidence, we induce in others, a faith in our ability.

Status

Insecurity potentially hinders our awareness or praise of the capabilities of others. We might refrain from paying tribute to others because of our constant attention to our own underlying emotions. Uncertainty leaves us craving to be the focus of attention. We may be threatened by another's competence.

It is probable that a mother-in-law may not listen to a daughter-in-law's advice because she fears being overshadowed. A daughter-in-law will not heed a mother-in-law's guidance because she senses intimidating counsel. If we trust our own potential, we can,

> "It is the trouble that never comes that causes the loss of sleep. "
>
> Charles Austin Bate

at times, permit others the opportunity to recommend guidance to us. This should leave us feeling stabilized, not undermined.

Apprehensive people most often assume others take ad-

> "If you want something very, very badly, let it go free. If it comes back to you, it's yours forever. If it doesn't it was never yours to begin with."
>
> Anonymous

vantage of them. In their anxiousness, they might presume they are laboring intensely, yet are possibly being taken advantage of. They are likely to investigate work ethics as they strive to be noticed and admired.

A mother-in-law or daughter-in-law might disparage each other's attempts to flourish, perhaps submerged in their own uncertainties. The mother-in-law and daughter-in-law are unjustified in their concern regarding how much they are valued by their son/husband. It is likely that the assessment the son/husband makes pertaining to his mother or wife fosters in them merit or demerit, whatever the case may be. These appraisals made by the son/husband credibly influence the value each woman places on herself. This is not potentially a positive thing for either woman to do to herself, nor should the son/husband bear the weight of this analysis. The mother and wife must appreciate their own importance based on their own judgments.

A husband's support of his wife encourages stability in the marriage. A son's reassurance to his mother decreases her fearfulness of losing her son. Developing your own self-esteem generates widespread benefits.

> "They can because they think they can."
>
> Virgil

Goals should be set and will probably compel us to direct our resources toward attaining those objectives. Schedules may have to change, and flexibility might become imperative. Mothers-in-law and daughters-in-law may appeal for a harmonious settlement.

Endless worrying about the reactions of others impedes a comfortable relationship between a mother-in-law and daughter-in-law. The consequences of too many assumptions can result in off-center conjectures. Deliberate before speaking and be attentive to what is expressed. Surmising another's motives can be burdensome. A mother-in-law and daughter-in-law should not want to jeopardize their affection for each other by considering conceivably unsound information.

> "The greatest thing in family life is to take a hint when a hint is intended, and not to take a hint when a hint isn't intended."
>
> Robert Frost

Trust

Sometimes mind games can become part of the scenario. It is difficult for anxious people to be receptive. They might expect it will be used against them. They limit their own involvement and the participation of others. Their sensitivity incites distrust. They view all people as competitors. Every person becomes a potential trickster, and credibility is nonexistent.

It is difficult to be friends with insecure people because they presume everyone wishes to outwit them. They are apprehensive of favors and skeptical of the intentions. They cannot relax their guard. It is difficult to nurture a relationship in such an atmosphere. Gaining a cynic's trust is difficult but not impossible. It preconditions patience and understanding as well as an acceptance of their cautious nature. Love and support produces affection and good will. Changing our attitudes rather than attempting to change the perspectives of others promotes growth.

Insecurity keeps a daughter-in-law silent. Insecurity will keep a mother-in-law fearful. Insecurity will keep both a mother-in-law and a daughter-in-law from communicating. Lack of communication between a mother-in-law and daughter-in-law will render the relationship meaningless and place the son/husband in the position of feasibly becoming the constant intermediary.

> *"To doubt everything or to believe everything are two equally convenient solutions; both dispense with the necessity of reflection."*
>
> Jules Henri

Building self-confidence makes one able to overlook many thoughtless remarks. It renders the ability to ascend intentional or unintentional hurt. Confidence in our abilities subdues controversial observations a mother-in-law and daughter-in-law discern. Disregarding tactless remarks instead of lashing out is the better course of action.

1st Vignette

Mary glanced at her watch. She wanted to prepare

> *"Challenges make you discover things about yourself that you never really knew. They're what make the instrument stretch—what makes you go beyond the norm".*
>
> *Cicely Tyson*

some plans for her meeting in the morning. It was getting late. Mary's eyes cut across the room to where Steve was sitting. Mary demanded Steve get the car, stating it was time to leave. Peg shot a look at the clock on the wall. It was still early. Peg steamed at her daughter-in-law's usual early departure. Peg was extremely agitated with the way her daughter-in-law, Mary, dominated her son, Steve. Just once, Peg wished Steve would speak for himself. Steve had been married to Mary for over twenty years. In all of those years, Steve learned that peace came with his submission to Mary. Steve noticed the disappointment in his mother's eyes, but he knew Mary must have wanted to hurry home to do something she considered important.

Peg learned to accept Mary's authoritative bearing toward Steve. Steve perpetually acquiesced. Peg resigned herself to her son's subordinate situation.

Mary never allowed Peg to enjoy time alone with her son. Mary was consistently present whenever Steve and Peg were conversing. Peg was cautious and prudent about every word she spoke to Steve. Whenever Peg invited her son and his

> *"Fear is a disease that eats away at logic and makes man inhuman."*
>
> *Marian Anderson*

family to dinner, Mary responded for all of them. Steve refrained from replying until he addressed the question to Mary. Peg laughed as she recalled one incident when she phoned her son at work and requested the family come to dinner. Her son expressed pleasure with this invitation, and Peg was delighted. That evening, Peg received a call from Steve who defaulted on the engagement. Peg cried and shook her head as she recollected the event. Peg learned quickly to appeal to Mary first and foremost.

Peg's grandchildren were currently in college. They were never allowed to visit their grandmother without their mother's presence. Mary insisted on supervising the visits. This system cultivated a distant relationship for Peg and her grandchildren. Peg received obligatory telephone calls and visits, but the relationship was deficient. Peg's grandchildren acted on cue rather than on their own emotions, which almost appeared to be masked. Spontaneity was gone, and the grandchildren were told where and when to say this or that. As the approach continued through adolescence and high school and college years, everyone got used to the manner, but Peg always felt deprived of a genuine emotion from her grandchildren. Sadly, Peg stated that now she never saw her grandchildren because

> "Throughout your life people will make you mad, disrespect you and treat you bad. Let God deal with the things they do, cause hate in your heart will consume you too."
>
> Will Smith

they moved far away from their parents and visited infrequently. Peg reflected that they had learned their lessons well and never looked back. She shook her head and said, "Their own mother now suffers their loss."

Peg recounted the time she sought to visit a grandchild at college. The university was close by. Peg extended a proposal for lunch. The young man seemed thrilled and accepted his grandmother's invitation. The day prior to the lunch date, Peg received a message from Mary. Mary spewed a profusion of excuses about why the lunch date had to be cancelled. She claimed the young man had exams and that it was an inopportune time. Mary stated that she was relaying the message for her son due to his stressful agenda. Peg sincerely noted and believed the proposal was declined because Mary uncovered the discreet overture. Peg relinquished in defeat.

> "The illiterate of the future will not be the person who cannot read. It will be the person who does not know how to learn."
>
> Alvin Toffler

1st Discussion

These relationships are fractured. Mary's fearfulness has kept Peg from the closeness to her grandchildren she desires. Trust as well as communication is necessary. Peg hungers to retain a connection with her son and daughter-in-law. She loves her daughter-in-law and her grandchildren, so she accepts all conditions.

> "Confidence, like art, never comes from having all the answers; it comes from being open to all the questions."
>
> Earl Gray Stevens

This is perhaps commendable, but not a solution. Adopting a subordinate arrangement discounts a healthy growth of actual love. The bonds exhibited by Mary and Peg are superficial. Honest connections of love and trust presumably were never allowed to grow and flourish.

Deeper feelings may be rewarded with an unfathomable sense of satisfaction. We might realize that there are many places in our hearts for love to grow and develop. Securing one tiny area in a grandchild, son, daughter, daughter-in-law, or son-in-law's heart should be more than acceptable and worthy of the effort. The infinite joy and everlasting imprint left on the heart will last forever. If our children can't learn to love others and forge connections to other family members, then when they are grown, they will not have any roots connecting them to any relatives. This could come back to bite everyone when there is nobody they care enough about to come back and see.

Allowing children to form relationships with relatives they easily communicate with is favorable. Having contacts with only one side of a family is shameful. Children are then deprived of all of the benefits that could possibly have been available to them.

> "For me growth begins immediately after I am able to admit my mistakes and forgive myself."
>
> Kimberly Kirberger

> *"Jealousy is the dragon which slays love under the pretense of keeping it alive."*
>
> *Havelock Ellis*

Parents need to ask themselves if what they are doing is beneficial to their child.

The apprehension Mary exhibits originates in her apprehension about sharing her children's love with other people. Her fears may be ungrounded, but they exist and fundamentally require attention. Ignoring distress does not allow one to escape the problem. Mary panics about what might be asserted in her absence. She withdraws in suspicion. Her children perpetuate her apprehension.

Peg's rapport with the grandchildren is illusive. It could improve if Mary realized there was enough love to share. The more we share love, the greater amount comes back to us. Steve might attempt to bolster Mary's self-confidence and, at the same time, request space for himself. Peg's sentiments could have been expressed openly. It is still possible for Peg and Mary to have a straightforward discussion. Peg merits a reprieve, and Mary warrants compassion amid surmounting stress. Peg deserves more than a fractured relationship with her grandchildren. She should do all in her power to change this situation. Peg could confront her son and request help in dealing with this problem. It is likely Peg may have to

> *"Hope is a good thing, maybe the best of things. And a good thing never dies."*
>
> *The Shawshank Redemption*

> "The truth of the matter is that you always know the right thing to do. The hard part is doing it."
>
> General H. Norman Schwarzkopf

challenge Mary and simply state her predicament. It is possible that Mary has never confronted her own fears and may not even realize that she has them.

2nd Vignette

Barbara is married to Charlie. She is a composed and confident woman. She and Charlie live in a condo, and both are pleased with the arrangement. She is quick to elude her contentedness as being novel.

Barbara recalled frail egos and vulnerability. When Barbara and Charlie were first married, they could not afford a house. They ventured a move into the first floor of a two-family house owned by Charlie's mother. Charlie's mother, Audrey, lived in the upstairs apartment. Audrey was kind and good-natured but domineering. She had complete control of her children during their childhoods. Audrey handled all the children's dilemmas.

Barbara and Charlie had a volatile marriage. When a fight ensued, Charlie would inevitably coerce his mother into the argument. Audrey consistently supported Charlie. Barbara admitted Charlie's mother disliked participating, but Charlie relentlessly managed to drag her

> "He who cannot forgive, breaks the bridge over which he himself must pass."
>
> George Herbert

into the disagreement. Charlie sensed his mother's reinforcement. Barbara lost the battle every time, and she suffered in silence during these quarrelsome episodes. Barbara had three children to raise and no place to go.

The circumstances remained unchanged as the children matured. Audrey always sustained Charlie. When the children were teenagers, they bought a dog. Audrey was annoyed. She did not appreciate a dog in the yard. Audrey eventually relinquished when pressured and allowed the children to keep the dog. Her one provision was they keep the yard clean. The children neglected the yard, and Audrey complained. A battle ensued between Audrey and her daughter-in-law. In a fit of anger, Audrey ordered Charlie and Barbara, along with their children, to leave the house.

> "We do not know, nor can we know, with absolute certainty, that those who disagree with us are wrong. We are human and therefore fallible and being fallible we cannot escape the element of doubt as to our own opinions and convictions."
>
> J. William Fulbright

Barbara was actually happy and relieved. Charlie was devastated. Barbara searched and rented a charming condo. She experienced freedom for the first time. Charlie was disoriented in the unfamiliar accommodations. He was displeased with his mother and irritable with his wife. A short while later, Audrey and Barbara amended their bonds. Their relationship was not perfect, but they were striving to improve it, and they were communicating.

2nd Discussion

Barbara and Charlie should have obtained a place of their own as soon as it was achievable. Audrey had an obligation to encourage her son's autonomy. Occupying the same house with one's parents likely undermines the couple by sustaining constant tension. It is possible that the parents may manipulate the adult child. It is also possible, as in this case, for the adult son to manipulate his mother involuntarily. It may be difficult to forego safeness, but when we renounce safety, we are rewarded with independence and a confidence in our own ability. The adult child should not fear venturing out on his or her own. We must forego refuge to gain self-reliance.

> "No one can make you feel inferior without your consent."
>
> Eleanor Roosevelt

Audrey erred in participating in the arguments between Charlie and Barbara. It was not Audrey's place to support either side during a dispute. The disagreement was between Barbara and Charlie. Audrey's opinion was not relevant or necessary.

Barbara was in a compromising position. Having young children, Barbara's options were limited. Barbara's precarious position was evident in the way she handled her anger. Barbara lashed out one minute and then would back down the next.

> "Our greatest glory is not in never failing, but in rising up every time we fail."
>
> Ralph Waldo Emerson

Charlie was secure with his mother's approval. Charlie's hesitation was in developing his own authority. His mother influenced all of his undertakings. It is imperative for Charlie to accept his wife as an equal and respect their marriage. Charlie needs to recognize his wife and children as separate entities from his childhood household.

Barbara was suppressed because of the insecure atmosphere. Barbara had no one to rely upon. Her options were few. Finding the courage to confront Audrey with her sentiments was one of Barbara's alternatives. Barbara had a right to voice her own opinions and be heard. Our vulnerabilities keep us at a standstill. Confronting them is an important first step in overcoming them. When we conquer our instability, we are capable of forming genuine bonds of communication and friendship. Worthiness enhances self-esteem, and our sense of worth and confidence in ourselves makes us less defensive and less offensive. Pride in our ability engenders security. This security

> "Confidence is a plant of slow growth. "
>
> Herbert V. Prochnow.

will allow us to reach out a hand in friendship rather than in battle. Our brightest glory comes from within the depths of our heart.

Reflections for Mothers-in-Law

New techniques evolve for the benefit of humanity. Concede the opportunity, permitting your daughter-in-law to experience advanced methods.

Provide approval.

Silence may be concealment for a lack of confidence and uncertainty. Encourage your daughter-in-law to express herself.

Accommodate your son and daughter-in-law. Empower them to take responsibility for their own lives.

Support your son and daughter-in-law's dreams. Dreams are necessary.

Champion your daughter-in-law's attempts rather than exerting your influence.

Negative remarks are destructive. Keep your words positive and constructive.

Reflections for Daughters-in-Law

Learning from past theories and mistakes fosters advancement.

Judge fairly, maintain your self-confidence, and be cognizant of the vulnerability in others.

Most questions do not have absolute answers.

Believe in the sweetness and innocence of vulnerability. Request help and admit doubt.

Be flexible. It will help maintain your sanity and allow you to see things in perspective.

Do not use your husband as a middleman when dealing with your mother-in-law. Overcome apprehensions of speaking with her yourself.

When you have reservations, arrange for additional reflection time.

Words spoken from the tips of tongues are not profound deliberations.

Questions for Mothers-in-Law

1. Are you afraid to say no when your daughter-in-law asks you to babysit?

   Always   Sometimes   Seldom

2. Do you make quick judgments about your daughter-in-law?

   Always   Sometimes   Seldom

3. Are you inflexible when plans change?

   Always   Sometimes   Seldom

4. Is your son impartial when you and your daughter-in-law disagree?

   Always   Sometimes   Seldom

5. Do any of your behaviors cause you guilt?

   Always   Sometimes   Seldom

6. Do your daughter-in-law's remarks provoke you?

   Always   Sometimes   Seldom

7. Are you critical of your daughter-in-law's cleaning, cooking, or child-rearing practices?

   Always   Sometimes   Seldom

8. Do you need the consent of others before making a decision?

   Always   Sometimes   Seldom

Questions for Daughters-in-Law

1. Is it distressing when your mother-in-law declines a babysitting request?

   Always   Sometimes   Seldom

2. Do you formulate quick judgments about your mother-in-law?

   Always   Sometimes   Seldom

3. Are you uncooperative when your mother-in-law alters your proposals?

   Always   Sometimes   Seldom

4. During a quarrel with your husband, does your mother-in-law render support to her son or remain neutral?

   Always   Sometimes   Seldom

5. Are you impelled to clarify your actions?

   Always   Sometimes   Seldom

6. Do contrary statements from your mother-in-law hamper you for an extended period?

   Always   Sometimes   Seldom

7. Are you intimidated to calculate a decision without another's confirmation?

   Always   Sometimes   Seldom

8 COMPETITION VS. COMPROMISE

Perhaps most people at one time or another contemplate their own imperfections and their strengths. Likely, they find it's easier to see the weaknesses in others. Feasibly, it is much simpler to perceive the failings of others more than we can appreciate our own. Being judgmental of our daughters-in-law or mothers-in-law generates the danger of alienating our daughters-in-law or distancing our mothers-in-law.

> "The more a man knows, the more he forgives."
>
> Catherine the Great

It is recommended that mothers-in-law refrain from articulating contrasting opinions about sons, daughters, sons-in-law, daughters-in-law, and grandchildren. The energy you put into these matters will merit the outcomes. Daughters-in-law need to desist from assuming that every insignificant remark spoken by their mothers-in-law is meant to be a rebuff against them.

> "There are glimpses of heaven to us in every act and thought or word that raises us above ourselves."
>
> A. P. Stanley

Some of us enjoy cooking. Others tolerate it. One daughter-in-law may cook gourmet meals served on a fancy tablecloth with a candle in the center, while another may buy boxed or frozen meals on the run served on paper plates. Some keep an orderly house, while most of us perhaps enjoy the lived-in look. Many mothers are busy tending to children as they bring them to Brownies, Cub Scouts, sports games, driving lessons, and numerous other activities.

How we choose to squander our free time can be distinctive. Being involved in groups and clubs and associations might leave us little time to clean house or tend to other chores. Those of us who are more private probably enjoy tranquil walks and time to read a good book.

Research shows that mothers-in-law and daughters-in-law dispute things such as pacifiers, toilet training, crawling, walking, height, weight, knowledge and learning, athletic ability, popularity, and the list goes on. A pacifier has become a sticking point between mothers-in-law and daughters-in-law. It has been called a crutch by some and to others a relief. Some mothers-in-law as well as some daughters-in-law attest to the advantage of the pacifiers. Many

> "Tolerance can lead to learning something."
>
> Jakob Dillon

"Reputation is what men and women think of us; character is what God and angels know of us."

Thomas Paine

children suck their thumbs or suck on a pacifier. How soon a bottle or pacifier or thumb is discontinued conveys the impression of an effective or inadequate mother.

Other items on the agenda include the mother who is the most environmentally conscious as well as knowledgeable about healthy foods and medicine. Although these are probably wonderful things to do, will it improve the essence of who we really are? A mother-in-law might be exceptionally tidy, while her daughter-in-law might have an active social life with modest time to clean. The reverse is also possible. A mother-in-law may have an extremely busy schedule and place little importance on mundane tasks. It is genuinely up to those specific people to decide for themselves what roles work for them. Criticism never operates in a supportive manner.

Another area of contention is bottle-feeding versus breast-feeding. There are countless pros and cons for both sides. The point is surely not which one has improved, but why mothers-in-law and daughters-in-law make it a competition about which one is the superior approach of performance. If the baby is thriving

"You have your way. I have my way. As for the right way, the correct way and the only way, it does not exist."

Friedrich Nietzsche

> "If you would know the road ahead, ask someone who has traveled it."
>
> Chinese proverb

and happy, then is it relevant what one prefers?

Scores of us believe we have more deficiencies than virtues, and perhaps this is why we project our aspirations on our children. When our children are prosperous, we feel victorious. We must remember that when our children reach the age of achieving success, we will not likely be the people they are thanking for their success.

At that point in time, they will most likely have a significant other who is supporting them and cheering

> "Some tension is good for the soul to grow, and we can put that intention to good use. We can look for every opportunity to give and receive love, to appreciate nature, to heal our wounds and the wounds of others, to forgive, and to serve.
>
> Joan Borysenko, from Handbook for the Soul

for them. The circle of life plays out again as daughters-in-law convert to becoming the mothers-in-law, who are then striving for the chance to spend time with their child or children.

Perhaps the question is why impose or wield your philosophies on others? None of this research is meant to make anybody be subjected to humiliation. On the contrary, we should celebrate our uniqueness, but not exploit it to offend or diminish another human being. People who are truly concerned with the latest research

> *"A child becomes an adult when he realizes that he has a right not only to be right but also to be wrong."*
>
> *Thomas Szasz*

and are sincere in their efforts and beliefs only become a problem when they cannot recognize or respect another's findings and beliefs that may be just as strong. It's good to remember that every generation is sure they have all of the answers.

In some cases, it is difficult to observe our sons interacting with their wives when they have scarcely any say in issues involving their homes or children. Likely, we remember those times when they were young children and nervous about speaking up. This is most likely not the case, but even if it were true, it is our son's responsibility to speak up. If he chooses to remain silent, we need to respect his choices and remember that if his relationship with his wife works, it should be left alone. This is difficult if a daughter-in-law proceeds to take advantage of this position and she shuts her mother-in-law out of her husband's world.

Most people turn out to be parents at some juncture in their lives, and so it appears unwise for one mother to want to deprive another mother of having a relationship with her child, even if he or she is now a grown-up. Perhaps men enjoy being taken care of and leave their mother's care for the care of their wives. Although a mother-in-law needs to get over

> *"To be wrong is nothing unless you continue to remember it."*
> *Confucius*

> "You must tolerate that which you cannot change."
>
> Spanish proverb

feelings of desertion, a daughter-in-law needs to be a big enough person to allow her mother-in-law some space to display care for her son. Just as a daughter enjoys her mother's pampering, so too does the son relish his mother's concern.

Most likely the competitiveness among mothers will remain but bonds of trust and appreciation can override any conflicts. We all rate our own performance on how accurately we succeed with a task. The more rapidly we perform, the more infatuated with ourselves we can become.

We all have varying needs and a distinctive threshold for pain, anxiety, and sensitivity. What functions for one child does not work for another. One child might be easier to soothe than another. One child may need more security than another. It is probable that all children will grow into productive adults, but at their own rate.

We do not have to make everything a competition. Growing up should not be formulated into a competition. Siblings compete somewhat as they grow, but parents ought to downplay this circumstance. If parents perceivably encourage this behavior, then it could possibly continue throughout adulthood and have an influence on the closeness of siblings.

> "Sure you can't put an old head on new shoulders."
>
> Bridget Kearney

> *"What you dislike in another take care to correct in yourself."*
>
> *Thomas Spratt*

Mothers-in-law might be guilty of these tactics, but what daughters-in-law need to be aware of is how it does not, and never will, affect how much they love their sons. It is true to say a mother-in-law does not really like one son any more than another son or daughter. This person grew inside of her for nine months and was raised by her. He is special to her and always will be. She may make awkward remarks, but she ultimately does not mean any maliciousness in them.

Mothers-in-law have also spent years being able to freely say whatever they entertained without having these comments scrutinized. Now it is essential that the mother-in-law watch what she says so that misinterpretations don't manifest. This can happen if a daughter-in-law chooses to interpret the mother-in-law's remarks for her husband, resulting in the closest thing to a disaster as anything could possibly be. It appears that daughters-in-law do not relate to the fact that this woman is the mother of this young man and that she loves him unconditionally.

> *"It requires less character to discover the fault of others than to tolerate them.*
>
> *J. Petit Senn*

Mothers-in-law may be completely unaware of the critique that their daughters-in-law are providing about them. A mother-in-law may persist in being completely blunt in her statements because she understands

> *"There is as much difference between the counsel that a friend giveth himself as there is between the counsel of a friend and a flatterer. For there is no such flatterer as a man's self."*
>
> *Francis Bacon*

her son appreciates her love for him. Doubt may enter when the daughter-in-law interprets what the mother-in-law says. As a rule of thumb, sons should do their own interpreting because they understand their own mothers and love them with all their heart.

Mothers-in-law and daughters-in-law who are more cognizant will not engage in this competitiveness. There are fluctuations and challenges that confront us every day. Some days we can pull more than our share of the load, while other days we cannot even pull our own portion.

If there is competition, then there will be a winner and a loser. The loser will walk away disgruntled and beaten. The loser may avoid contact with the winner and the person who set up the competition.

One must be reminded that sometimes we create our own competition. It may not always be the mother-in-law or the daughter-in-law causing it. The mother-in-law or daughter-in-law could become the scapegoat, but they may be innocent.

> *"Success is the sum of small efforts repeated day in and day out."*
>
> *Robert Collier*

When a mother-in-law compliments another sibling or

grandchild or daughter, the daughter-in-law cannot interpret this as a format for a rivalry. Every time a daughter-in-law shares the most recent event in her young child's life does not mean she is boastful.

Arranging for adult children to be competitive will likely cause anger, frustration, and guilt. Be cognizant of the fact that all children can be depended upon to carry out distinct undertakings. Some children are prodigious at inviting their parents for dinner and entertaining them. Other children are present when there is a difficulty. Still others will assume major responsibilities for their parents if the time and need arises. Love should not be built on necessity or dependability. Genuine love is unconditional and perpetual to all participants at all times.

> "Mistakes are a part of being human.
> Appreciate your mistakes for what they are: precious life lessons that can only be learned the hard way. Unless it's a fatal mistake, which, at least others can learn from. "
>
> Al Franken

1st Vignette

Kara enjoyed the company of Amanda. Both women got along well together. They each had a four-year-old son, and Kara also had a two-year-old son, while Amanda had a two-year-old daughter. Kara and Amanda were married to two brothers named Kevin and Dan.

There was only one problem in their relationship and that was their mother-in-law, Gail. She was kind

> "Divide the fire and you will soon put it out."
>
> Greek proverb

and helpful, but Gail never ceased to get Kara upset with her remarks.

Kara's four-year-old son, Jim, was of average height for his age, but he was thin. Amanda's son, Tim, was about the same height, but broader and larger boned. Jim and Tim played well together, but Gail ceaselessly commented on Tim's larger size. Gail equated size with ability and strength. Gail unconsciously interacted more with Tim because she was amused with his bulk. Jim was just as strong, if not stronger, but being slight, he did not attract Gail's attention.

Kara tried to control her anger, but it was challenging. Jim and Tim were the same height, but when Gail would talk to a friend or another family member, she would always say Tim was taller. Gail would also mention that Tim was going to be a big man. Gail never mentioned Jim.

Kara couldn't conceive of Gail's predictions. It amazed Kara that Gail felt she had the right to even formulate them. Kara was defenseless. If she tried to say anything, it would be like sour grapes. Kara didn't care if Jim was shorter when he was grown. What bothered her was her mother-in-law's equating size with being

> "The highest reward for a person's toil, is not what they get for it but what they become by it."
>
> John Rushkin

better.

1st Discussion

Gail unquestionably was causing frustration and turmoil for herself through all of her comments about her grandchildren and children. Pitting siblings or grandchildren against each other creates animosity and tension. There must be a winner, and therefore, there must be a loser.

> "When you get into a tight place and everything goes against you, till it seems as though you could not hang on a minute longer, never give up then, for that is just the place and time that the tide will turn."
>
> Harriet Beecher Stowe

Gail is unwittingly causing a rift between Kara and Amanda. They have a nice relationship, and they are married to two brothers. If Kara has had enough, then she will stay away from Amanda and Gail, and this would be sad for all of them.

How do any of us think we have the right to judge another person? With girls, beauty might become another area that causes suffering. Many sisters, as well as sisters-in-law, are compared. Grandchildren can also be compared. How do we decide what beauty is or is not? At times, competition leads to opposition, strife, and combativeness. Good friends or relatives can become rivals and enemies. Look for the outstanding attributes in everyone because they are there. You might just have to look harder or longer for some.

2ⁿᵈ Vignette

Victoria was married to Gina's son, Lucas. Gina also had three grown daughters. Victoria and Lucas were also raising three daughters of their own. Gina tried hard to keep up with pleasing her daughter-in-law and her own three daughters, which was no small task. Her daughters often requested her help, and she was always willing to provide assistance. Victoria never asked for help, but she would always take notice of something Gina had done for one of her daughters.

> "To err is human; to admit it, superhuman."
>
> Doug Larson

Gina was an expert knitter. She knitted mittens and hats and scarves for all of her grandchildren. All of them had received at least one sweater—at least that's what Gina thought. If given a request, she always tried to reply in the affirmative. Many times, she just threw out offers to help. "If you need a babysitter," she would say, "I'm available."

Victoria, Gina noticed, was always friendly when the two of them were alone, but never when there were others around. Gina recalled times when Victoria was almost rude to her, but when all the company had left, Victoria talked to Gina like they were old friends. Victoria rarely called Gina, but Gina made excuses for her, rationalizing that she was probably busy.

> "Out of suffering have emerged the strongest souls. The most massive characters are seared with scars."
>
> E .H Chapin

Gina always brooded over just how much Victoria liked her. It was as if Victoria resented Gina for not helping, yet Victoria always refused any offers of help that Gina gave. As Gina got older, her daughter-in-law commented one day that her youngest daughter, Caitlin, never got a hand-knitted sweater. Gina felt horrible about this. She, in good conscience, thought she had knitted sweaters for all of her grandchildren.

Gina couldn't forget the expression on her granddaughter's face when Victoria made the comment. Victoria felt justified with her actions and went on to state how daughters are daughters and daughters-in-law are just daughters-in- law. Victoria had a wide smile on her face, but not one that gave the impression of someone who was happy. The smile registered no crinkles at the corners of her eyes.

Gina had prided herself in always being fail-safe. Now she was beside herself with worry. Her husband, Joe, tried to calm her down. Joe had observed over the

> "Good people are good because they've come to wisdom through failure.
>
> William Saroyan

years, the thoughtful gifts Gina bought for Victoria. The gifts Gina received in return were impersonal. This conversation didn't help Gina, and tears were now streaming down her face, and her sobs were uncontrollable. She concluded that mothers-in-law make daughters-in-law mad, but daughters-in-law make mothers-in-law sad.

Joe put his arms around Gina and held her tightly. "I love you, Gina, and I know you on the inside. You would never intentionally hurt any of them," Joe remarked.

"Yeah, Joe, but Caitlyn probably thinks I don't love her as much," Gina replied.

"Look at it this way, Gina. If it wasn't this, it would've been something else."

Gina shook her head. Neither she nor Joe slept that night.

2nd Discussion

Victoria expected her mom to indulge her more than she indulged her son's wife, yet she expected her mother-in-law to play fair. Gina had always tried to do this, but when the games and rules get switched repeatedly, a person becomes predestined to lose. After reflecting on the situation, Gina remembered that her fingers were getting very arthritic when Caitlyn was born. She complained to her daughters, and they told her not to worry about knitting a sweater. They would give their mother's hand-knitted sweaters to Victoria, as their daughters were too big for a lot of the sweaters. Gina was happy and thought everything was satisfactory. Now she understood that it wasn't, and she could not retrieve the years.

> *"Shallow men believe in luck. Strong men believe in cause and effect."*
>
> *Ralph Waldo Emerson*

There was no way she could knit a sweater now. Maybe her friend Rose would do it for her. She would pay her. Gina felt better already. Victoria alleged that Gina favored her daughters. She stated it countless times, and even Gina's son, Lucas, accepted it as truth. Of course, Gina knew this was not accurate, but she was an amateur when dealing with her daughter-in-law, Victoria. All of Gina's efforts in trying to be the most perfect mother-in-law that she could be backfired. The more arduous attempts Gina made, the more Victoria wanted to establish her deficiencies. What Victoria didn't know was the problem Gina had with arthritis. Gina's health wasn't discussed often because no one asked, and if they did, it was strictly out of courtesy because no one ever let her finish before moving on to another topic. Gina got in the habit of stating everything was just fine.

Reflections for Mothers-in-Law

Try to refrain from comparing your children and grandchildren.

Remember that we all need more support than we do critics.

Overlook any flaws you see in others and focus solely on their attributes.

Keep in mind what the best attributes actually are.

Recall those days when you were new at experiencing motherhood and being a new bride.

Understand that in the mother-in-law and daughter-in-law relationship you are the parent. You have already trodden the path. You should be able to avoid the potholes.

Life is short like a candle's life. Try to keep yours glowing bright as you guide the way for others, without burning them in the process.

Reflections for Daughters-in-Law

Try not to perceive every situation with your mother-in-law as a competition.

Whether or not you win or lose a rivalry with your mother-in-law will not mean anything a few years into the future.

Competing with any other person is nonsense because it is just not relevant in the grand scheme of life.

Life is short like a candle's life, try to keep yours glowing bright as you guide the way for others, without burning them in the process.

Remember that we all need more support than critics.

Refrain from comparing your mother-in-law to your mother.

Questions for Mothers-in-Law

1. Do you like to prove to your daughter-in-law that you were more efficient at handling your children than she appears to be with hers?

   Always   Sometimes   Seldom

2. Are you always making comments about what your daughter-in-law is doing?

   Always   Sometimes   Seldom

3. Do you have a negative attitude about things your daughter-in-law gets excited about?

   Always   Sometimes   Seldom

4. Do you ever let your daughter-in-law know that you respect her and believe she is doing something better than you did yourself?

   Always   Sometimes   Seldom

5. Do you consider your daughter-in-law's ideas to be more of a fad?

   Always   Sometimes   Seldom

Questions for Daughters-in-Law

1. Do you look down on all of your mother-in-law's ways of doing things?

   Always   Sometimes   Seldom

2. Do you consider your mother-in-law's ideas old fashioned and out of date?

   Always   Sometimes   Seldom

3. Do you make your mother-in-law feel like she was profusely wrong when she was raising your husband?

   Always   Sometimes   Seldom

4. Do you ever compliment your mother-in-law for a job well done?

   Always   Sometimes   Seldom

5. Do you deliberately embarrass your mother-in-law in front of her son?

   Always   Sometimes   Seldom

9 TOLERANCE

Interference causes conflict between a mother-in-law and daughter-in-law. Most of us do not like unsolicited advice. Most of us only request advice from those who are quick to agree with us. When we say we are searching for another view, we are perhaps really scanning for confirmation.

> "To be wrong is nothing unless you continue to remember it."
>
> Confucius

If a son asks his mother for advice, it is likely going to be considered meddling by the daughter-in-law. She does not have the same faith and confidence in his mother and may resent any counsel offered.

The person giving advice is most likely the sovereignty figure. A daughter-in-law does not want to see her mother-in-law in a position of power. Conceivably, following somebody's advice is the equivalent of granting them control over you and your decisions. If a son takes his mother's advice and things work out, then the mother should not dwell on it. Mothers-in-law must

> "Our greatest glory consists not in never falling but in rising every time we fall."
>
> Oliver Goldsmith

> "Each time something difficult and challenging has happened to me it has marked the beginning of a new era in my life."
>
> Kimberly Kirberger

learn how to gracefully impart their knowledge and leadership and then bow out of the situation.

On the contrary, accepting guidance never made anyone a fool, yet we should always trust our own judgment in the final analysis. Perceivably, if we are secure, then listening to someone else's counsel should not make us feel incompetent. A daughter-in-law might feel threatened to some degree if her mother-in-law were consistently interfering in the belief that her daughter-in-law is young and inexperienced. Even if her advice is excellent, it may be unwanted. A couple has an obligation to acquire answers for themselves.

If a mother-in-law comes to realize that what worked for her and her husband may not work or be correct for her son and daughter-in-law, she will back off and allow the couple to make their own decisions. They may make mistakes, but they will learn together.

Many mothers-in-law think that by pointing out

> "We seldom confide in those who are better than ourselves."
>
> Albert Camus

their daughter-in-law's faults to their sons they are doing them a favor. Your son will think less of you. Your daughter-in-law is not you, and you can't anticipate that she will measure up to your ex-

> *"Courage is doing what you're afraid to do. There can be no courage unless you're scared."*
>
> *Eddie Rickenbacker*

pectations. If you demand too much of your daughter-in-law, you will push her and your son away. If a mother-in-law demonstrates a more relaxed attitude, then she will have lightened her daughter-in-law's fears about doing a poor job.

A good rule to keep is to remain silent when the couple is making decisions. Allow them to allocate and distribute household chores. If we believe that our sons should be able to come home to a home-cooked meal, but then we see them starting the supper, we should input nothing. Maybe your daughter-in-law's job is more stressful. Maybe your son gets home first. If your son is not complaining, then you shouldn't, either.

There is a fine line between guiding a child and acting out the parent-child relationship. We must remember that we are dealing with adults. If we were consulted on one subject, that does not give us the authority to voice an opinion on every matter pertaining to the couple. We do not have the permission to keep offering opinions.

> *"Only those who do nothing at all make no mistakes but that would be a mistake."*
>
> *Anonymous*

Tolerance might mean accepting a mother-in-law or a daughter-in-law who is reasonably dissimilar from us. She might have grown up in a different ethnic culture, economic

> *"The best rose bush after all is not that which has the fewest thorns but that which bears the finest roses."*
>
> *Henry Van Dyke*

home, or with a completely different set of rules. Whatever the case may be, we need to assess the common bonds that we have and focus on those. In many ways, we might find we are more alike than different.

One daughter-in-law has so many rules that her mother-in-law is afraid to take any action without checking first if it is okay to do it, while another daughter-in-law recalled how she drove her mother-in-law crazy with her lack of rules for her children. She was a free spirit and allowed her children to literally eat at any time of the day or night and, likewise, put themselves to bed whenever they were tired. There were no rules. Other than the fact she could never get a babysitter to sit more than once, she and her husband and children were extremely happy. She is now the proud grandmother of many grandchildren and is currently driving her daughter-in-law as crazy as she caused her mother-in-law to be years ago.

Silence may alleviate many problems. In the circle of life, we will most likely play both roles of daughter-

> *"The more a man knows, the more he forgives."*
>
> *Catherine the Great*

in-law and mother-in-law. If we comprehend this fact, then we should put greater effort into all of us getting along.

1st Vignette

> "Peace cannot be kept by force, it can only be achieved by understanding."
>
> Albert Einstein

Phyllis was a new grandmother. She was excited for her son and daughter-in-law, but felt she was always doing the wrong thing. I questioned her further, and she revealed her side of the story:

"My daughter-in-law, Mckenna, goes to school part time to finish her four-year degree. She only goes on Tuesdays. That's the night my son, Stan, is in charge of Jenny, their baby daughter. Stan leaves work early. When Mckenna first started school, Stan was nervous because Jenny would cry a lot. He began coming over to the house regularly, and to tell you the truth, I just loved seeing both of them. I would rock Jenny until she fell off to sleep, and then Scott, my husband, and I and Stan would sit down to a nice meal like we used to before Stan was married.

"I told Stan to just come over on Tuesdays, and we

> "Any intelligent fool can make things bigger, more complex, and more violent. It takes a touch of genius and a lot of courage to move in the opposite direction."
>
> Albert Einstein.

could all eat supper. It went okay until Mckenna found out that Stan and Jenny were coming. I must admit that I thought Mckenna knew about the arrangement, but apparently Stan never told Mckenna about it. I could not understand Mckenna's reaction. She called my son immature and incapable of watching his daughter. She was so an-

> "Who seeks a quarrel will find it near at hand."
>
> *Italian proverb*

gry that Stan stopped coming. I don't know what my daughter-in-law was trying to prove, but she just made all of us unhappy.

"My son works full time and he gets tired after a long day at work. I didn't mind watching Jenny. My daughter-in-law only works part time because she goes to school. I just cannot figure it out. Now my son barely talks to me about anything. I know there are times when Mckenna needs to study, and she ventures over to her mother's house and lets her mother watch the baby. Why can she have help from her mother and it's not immature, but Stan can't have any help from his mother?"

I didn't have answers to Phyllis's plight. Perhaps in the mother-in-law and daughter-in-law dilemma, there is a double standard.

1st Discussion

I was very sorry for Phyllis because she could not perceive where she was going wrong. She was acting decently, but she did not grasp her mistakes. There are some daughters-in-law who would not be concerned by such an arrangement, but apparently Phyllis and Mckenna had an interference problem.

Mckenna did not feel that Phyllis was assisting her in any way. She alleged that it was Stan's job to provide care for his own child. In Mckenna's eyes, he was shirking his responsibilities by requesting the help of

> *"Blessed are the hearts that can bend, they shall never be broken."*
>
> *Albert Camus*

his mother. If Stan had gone to his mother's once or twice, Mckenna probably would not have been angry.

Phyllis may have done a nobler service to both her son and daughter-in-law if she had invited both of them over with the baby. Mckenna obviously was not getting the respite that Stan was getting, which was probably most of the problem. Because Stan's watch for Jenny was limited, Mckenna sensed Stan should be taking care of Jenny. Phyllis was not aware of the fact that she was interfering with Stan's fatherly obligations and possibly slighting Mckenna. Phyllis was not allowing her son to be a father in Mckenna's eyes. The one night he was in charge, he was relegating his duties to his mother.

Mckenna could have talked to Stan and requested that he stay home more often and visit his mother only once in a while rather than get everyone involved and upset. Mckenna could have tried to explain her point of view or allowed Stan to have the break with

> *" Not everything that counts can be counted and not everything that can be counted counts"*
>
> *Albert Einstein*

his mother and then request his help at another time. Stan would likely be more apt to help her at another time because he was aware of the help he was receiving from his mother. Mckenna also should have been able to talk things over and work something out. Phyllis could have made a to-go dinner for her daughter-in-law and possibly gained her respect and affection. Mothers-in-law can feasibly help, and might offer to help, but they should not interfere or set patterns without the approval of both their son and daughter-in-law. Sons must stand on their own feet. Daughters-in-law should recognize, though, that their husbands might need a break once in a while. Allowing a son to lean on his mother does not necessarily mean he is incapable. He might simply need and want a breather.

> "In a moment of decision the best thing you can do is the right thing. The worst thing you can do is nothing."
>
> Theodore Roosevelt

2nd Vignette

Lilly and Ryan were married for five years. Lilly worked hard at her job as a computer analyst. It never gave her much time to be outside or get some fresh air. Ryan suggested they go away for a weekend to a beach area. Lilly debated this offer. She really wanted to go, and she knew that Ryan wanted to go, but they had been working so hard to save for a down payment on a house. After a difficult day, Lilly relented and agreed that it was a great idea.

It was an impressive plan until Babette, Ryan's mother, found out about it. She convinced Ryan that it was frivolous to spend the money in this manner. She stated that the weekend would pass by fast, but having a house would be forever. Ryan went home to

Lilly with his doubts.

Lilly was furious. She admitted that it was a bit frivolous, but she sensed that it was a mini vacation that they both needed. She couldn't understand Ryan's change in attitude after talking with his mother. They fought about it, and then Ryan agreed to go, but Lilly cancelled the whole vacation. The couple was hardly speaking by that point.

2nd Discussion

Babette, of course, played a terrible role in this whole scenario. One must remember, though, that Babette is one person. She could not force the couple into doing anything. The guilt for Babette lay in the fact that she openly voiced an opinion to her son. Ryan was obviously questioning if this idea was a good one or a bad one. Ryan told his mother and, in the process, requested her opinion, which he never should have done. Ryan should have been more steadfast in his decision to take a vacation. Lilly should also have been more adamant about going. Lilly could have told Babette how much she needed to get away and how important it was to her and Ryan. If her mother-in-law was not moved, then Lilly should have stated that she wanted to go and would go.

> *"Opportunity... often it comes in the form of misfortune, or temporary defeat."*
>
> *Napoleon Hill*

> "We can't solve problems by using the same kind of thinking we used when we created them."
>
> Albert Einstein

Ryan and Lilly planned the trip. Babette should not have ventured an opinion. How a couple chooses to spend their money is up to them. If they waste it, they face the consequences. If they save or throw it away, it is only their business. Ryan should not have been so easily swayed by his mother. What a mother-in-law sees as essential and what a daughter-in-law and her husband see as vital can vary a great deal.

One couple I know sought to travel around the world and live in hostels and camps. They both quit their jobs and journeyed for one year. Both sets of parents thought they had lost their way. The couple came back home refreshed and renewed. They acquired good jobs. Today, they are part of mainstream society, but have wonderful stories to tell about their past escapades. What all of us need and desire is different. We must be allowed to do our own thing without anyone intruding on our dreams.

> "Treat all the people you meet each day as though it were their last day on earth."
>
> The Grain and Feed Merchant.

3rd Vignette

Doris had three sons and no daughters. All three of her sons were married. She was always worried when the holidays came around because she was never sure who might invite her and her husband, Jim, for dinner. Doris loved entertaining, but in recent years, her daughters-in-law wanted to make their own plans. The problems arose when Doris was not included in their plans and wasn't invited anyplace. She began to feel as though she was just an afterthought, but she quickly pushed these negative opinions aside. She concentrated on what to cook for Christmas dinner for two.

Suddenly, her middle son, Andrew, called and invited them to dinner. Doris was thrilled but nervous. Sharon, her daughter-in-law, was always cooking things Doris didn't enjoy eating. She would say it was her family tradition. In Doris's mind, it was always her daughter-in-law's family traditions and never about her son Andrew's.

> "Don't walk in front of me, I may not follow. Don't walk behind me, I may not lead. Walk beside me and be my friend."
>
> Albert Camus

Doris was amazed how Andrew appeared to be gobbled up and absorbed into their family. Somehow Doris and her husband were left behind. Andrew had discarded all of the traditions he had grown up with. When entering their home, pictures of Sharon's side of the family were prominently displayed, yet none of Andrew's brothers were framed on any wall. Doris made up her mind to bite her tongue and refrain from any negative remarks, not that she ever would speak negatively, but she would make an extra effort to taste the various dishes her

> "The opposite of love is not hate but indifference."
>
> Elie Wiesel

daughter-in-law made. After all, her daughter-in-law was kind enough to invite her.

Doris and Jim were quiet people, as was their son Andrew. Sharon and her family were boisterous, and at times, it was hard to tell if they were arguing or just enjoying a conversation. When the holiday arrived, Doris and Jim approached the entrance to Andrew's home. Their son greeted his parents and escorted them to the den. Sharon called to Andrew for help in the kitchen. Doris's offers of help were declined, so Doris and Jim talked quietly to each other.

Upon the arrival of Sharon's family, which consisted of her parents and three siblings, the room was bouncing with noise and laughter. Doris was hugged and kissed by all and then left alone to sit by herself. Doris and Jim and the rest of the guests were called to the dinner table within an hour. Everyone helped themselves, and plates were being passed around every which way. Doris got tired of asking what each dish was as it juggled by. Doris and Jim ate very little, but no one seemed to notice.

Drowned out by all the buzzing talk, Doris and Jim caught tidbits of conversations from various areas of the room. As the day came to a close, Doris and Jim said their good-byes to Andrew and Sharon. Andrew

> "We only know of one duty and that is to love."
>
> Albert Camus

kissed his mother, saying, "I hope you had a good time?" Doris smiled and nodded her head saying thank you both. In the car, Doris leaned her head back on the car seat and closed her eyes. She didn't want to talk about the day and hoped Jim had enjoyed it more than she had.

Jim was quiet, and it was hard for Doris to read him. Upon their arrival at home, there were messages of Merry Christmas from her other two sons. Unexpectedly, tears gently streamed down Doris's face without any noise. Doris was confused, and she didn't understand why. She didn't even know how it happened, but she had completely lost all connections to her sons. It was as if she wasn't real to them anymore. Doris had no options. She stoically went to bed, but couldn't fall asleep. Jim and Doris stayed awake for a long time before finally being engulfed in a deep sleep.

3rd Discussion

Obviously, Doris is most likely reminiscing too much about holidays of the past. Those are gone, and new memories need to be made. Doris is a gentle soul and doesn't like to create any scenes, but she really should share some of her likes and dislikes with her daughters-in-law. She definitely needs to be more assertive. Possibly taking over a conversation might have been good for Doris and Jim as they ingratiated themselves into the conversations. We all have our own needs. Doris and Jim might also think about having a shared get together after the holiday. This might allow all of her sons to be there and allow Doris and Jim to visit with their sons in a peaceful, quiet manner. Doris would not feel so lost at a holiday gathering again if she was aware that she would have the chance to experience her own holiday time. Andrew and Sharon were kind to invite Doris and Jim, but they could have gone further by ensuring that both were comfortable.

"People are unreasonable, illogical and self-centered. Love them anyway.

If you do good, people accuse you of selfish, ulterior motives. Do good anyway.

If you are successful, you will win false friends and true enemies. Succeed anyway

The good you do today will be forgotten tomorrow. Do good anyway.

Honesty and frankness make you vulnerable. Be honest and frank anyway.

The biggest person with the biggest ideas can be shot down by the smallest person with the smallest mind. Think big anyway.

What you spend years building may be destroyed overnight. Build it anyway.

People really need help but may attack if you help them. Help people anyway.

Give the world the best you have and you might get kicked in the teeth. Give the world the best you've got anyway. "

Anonymous

Reflections for Mothers-in-Law

Do grant your son and daughter-in-law lots of space, and offer little advice even when you are asked.

Do give lots of praise and encouragement. Hold back on the interference.

Do stay neutral when your son and daughter-in-law are having a dispute.

Do accept your daughter-in-law's personality type. Allow her to be herself.

Do tolerate your daughter-in-law's beliefs expressed in the presence of others, even if you do not agree with them.

Do tolerate your daughter-in-law's style.

Reflections for Daughters-in-Law

Do respect your mother-in-law's advice without feeling pressured to follow it.

Do express your appreciation to your mother-in-law when she remains neutral during a dispute with your husband.

Do accept your mother-in-law's personality type. Allow her to be herself.

Do tolerate your mother-in-law's beliefs expressed in the presence of others, even when you do not agree with them.

Do remember your mother-in-law must have done something right in child rearing because you fell in love with her son.

Questions for Mothers-in-Law

1. Do you communicate with your son only?

    Always   Sometimes   Seldom

2. Do you include your daughter-in-law in your discussions?

    Always   Sometimes   Seldom

3. Do you tell your son and daughter-in-law how to spend their time, money, or vacation?

    Always   Sometimes   Seldom

4. Are you critical of your daughter-in-law's style of clothing?

    Always   Sometimes   Seldom

5. Are you critical of your daughter-in-law's child-rearing practice?

    Always   Sometimes   Seldom

6. Do you act like a reporter when your son and daughter-in-law visit?

    Always   Sometimes   Seldom

7. Do you listen to your son complain about his wife when they have recently argued?

    Always   Sometimes   Seldom

8. Do you worry about what your daughter-in-law might say when she is around your friends?

   Always   Sometimes   Seldom

9. Are you disappointed with your daughter-in-law's style of clothing when you attend certain functions?

   Always   Sometimes   Seldom

Questions for Daughters-in-Law

1. Do you assume that every time your mother-in-law makes a suggestion, she is intruding?

   Always   Sometimes   Seldom

2. Do you deduce that your mother-in-law is prying every time she asks a question?

   Always   Sometimes   Seldom

3. Do you expect your mother-in-law to invite you for dinner without ever reciprocating because; after all, she wants to see her son?

   Always   Sometimes   Seldom

4. Do you expect your mother-in-law to change her plans if you need a favor done?

   Always   Sometimes   Seldom

5. Do you get angry at your mother-in-law's questions, even when she is simply interested in a caring way?

   Always   Sometimes   Seldom

6. Do you ignore your mother-in-law when your friends are present?

   Always   Sometimes   Seldom

7. When your mother-in-law makes a suggestion, do you always assume she is being meddlesome?

   Always   Sometimes   Seldom

8. Do you stop to think and respect your mother-in-law's silence when you and your husband are fighting?

   Always   Sometimes   Seldom

Tolerance

10 CHILDREN & GRANDCHILDREN

"To My Children

Dear firstborn
I've always loved you best because you were our
first miracle. You were the genesis of a marriage
and the fulfillment of young love. You sustained us
through the hamburger years, the first apartment
(furnished in early poverty) our first mode of
transportation and the seven-inch TV we paid on
for 36 months. You were new, had unused
grandparents and enough clothes for a set of
triplets. You were the original model for a mom
and dad who were trying to work the bugs out.
You got the strained lamb, the open safety pins
and three hour naps. You were the beginning.

Dear Middle Child
I've always loved you best because you drew a tough
spot in the family and it made you stronger for it.
You cried less, had more patience, wore faded hand
me downs and never in your life did anything first.
But it only made you more special. You were the one
we relaxed with, who helped us realize a dog could
kiss you and you wouldn't get sick. You could cross a
street by yourself long before you were old enough
to get married. And you helped us understand the
world wouldn't collapse if you went to bed with dirty
feet. You were the child of our busy ambitious years.
Without you we never could have survived the job
changes and the tedium and routine that is
marriage."

"To The Baby:
I've always loved you best because while endings are
generally sad you are such a joy. You readily
accepted the milk-stained bibs, the lower bunk the
cracked baseball bat, the baby book that had
nothing written in it except a recipe for graham
cracker pie crust that someone had jammed
between the pages. You are the one we held on to so
tightly. You are the link with our past, a reason for
tomorrow. You darken our hair, quicken our steps,
square our shoulders, restore our vision and give us
a sense of humor that security, maturity and
durability can't provide. When your hairline takes on
the shape of Lake Erie and your own children tower
over you, you will still be our baby."
Anonymous

When a new baby is expected, there are many changes taking place. All those involved need time to adjust. The new parents are about to learn the meaning of loyalty, love, sacrifice, and giving without receiving.

Motherhood is universal. All mothers can understand the highs and lows. This can and should create a common bond between the mother-in-law and daughter-in-law. But this may also cause friction. A new baby generates upheaval upon its arrival but can also promote a peaceful atmosphere. One thing is assured: Things will never be the same for anybody involved.

Childcare is essential with the birth of a child. Many grandparents who are within a car's ride are solicited to babysit. Babysitting for grandchildren has its advantages and disadvantages. Although on the surface it might be appealing to spend so much time with the grandchildren, it might end up becoming a minefield.

> " If your baby is " beautiful and perfect, and never cries or fusses, sleeps on schedule and burps on demand, an angel all the time", you're the grandma."
>
> Teresa Bloomingdale

Overstepping your authority with your grandchildren or complaining about them are but a few of the risks. There is a fine line between visiting with versus babysitting your grandchild. The same rules need to apply.

You must not offer unsolicited advice or ignore your daughter-in-law's instructions; this would be

211

"I'd rather be a mother than anyone on Earth.,
Bringing up a child or two of unpretentious birth.
I'd rather nurse a rosy babe with warm lips on my breast.
Than wear a queen's medallion above a heart less blest.
I'd rather tuck a little child all safe and sound in bed.
Than twine a chain of diamonds about my foolish head.
I'd rather wash a smudgy face with round, bright baby eyes.
Than paint the pageantry of fame or walk among the wise."
By Meredith Gray

more than folly. Know your place. A daughter-in-law who is expecting her mother-in-law to be the regular daily care provider should relax her attitude and muster some appreciation for the time and effort that cannot be repaid. You need to acknowledge the fact that babysitting is not the same as visiting. Your mother-in-law is working. Likely, she is in a situation where she will lose no matter which way she chooses. If she complains, she risks her daughter-in-law's assumption that she doesn't love her grandchildren or doesn't like to see them or babysit them. If she agrees to babysit daily, she might become exhausted and burnt out but afraid to complain. To think she loves to babysit for you every day and in the process give up her free time and duties is an absurd assumption. Appreciation is gladly welcomed.

Some mothers-in-law are ready willing and able to take care of their grandchildren and

> *"I bend but I do not break."*
>
> *Jean de La Fontaine*

want to do this. Again, we are all different. But the same rules need to apply because you still face the possibility of issues as time passes. All grandmothers love their grandchildren. All grandmothers enjoy them and want to see them. It would be hurtful for a daughter-in-law to use this as a tool of punishment against the grandmother. Evidence exists that a poor relationship between a daughter-in-law and her mother-in-law will reflect the relationship between a grandmother and her grandchildren. Assuming your children can have a productive relationship with their grandmother even if you do not have one with your mother-in-law will likely prove you wrong in years to come. Maintaining the relationship between a mother-in-law and daughter-in-law is potentially paramount to keeping the relationship between grandchildren and their grandmothers.

Considerations for Mothers-in-Law

Just because a mother-in-law has experienced motherhood and child rearing does not necessarily make her an expert. A mother-in-law cannot assume her alleged expertise in the matter will be acknowledged by her daughter-in-law. From the beginning of a pregnancy, a daughter-in-law may distance herself from advice and opinions. This is her pre-

> *"To understand your parent's love you must raise children yourself."*
>
> *Chinese Proverb*

rogative. A mother-in-law does not want to detract from her daughter-in-law's experience with compulsory advice. Unsolicited opinions foster disharmony, even when the counsel is worthy. Caution should be heeded with solicited advice. Keep within the boundaries of impartiality.

New ideas and experiments are on the market every day. Your daughter-in-law may decide to take a chance on a new concept. Her judgment necessitates your deference. By supporting your daughter-in-law, you viably enhance her security and lessen the friction between you and her. Exploring new methods leads to research and proficiency.

> "Human beings are perhaps never more frightening than when they are convinced beyond doubt that they are right."
>
> Laurens Van der

If your daughter-in-law trusts you, she will confide in you and allow you to care for her child. Following the mother's lead will ensure less antagonism. A mother-in-law should not become an adversary to the daughter-in-law. The daughter-in-law has the authority to set the rules for television time, bedtime, eating, snacking, and boundaries for safety.

A mother-in-law who recognizes the authority of her daughter-in-law will bend to her daughter-in-law's requests. This creates assurance and a relaxed atmosphere.

A mother-in-law who does not follow the orders

set by her daughter-in-law runs the risk of not having access to her grandchildren. Trust and honesty is important in a mother-in-law and daughter-in-law's relationship, as it is in any association. A mother-in-law might ask for small courtesies and concessions. The daughter-in-law might grant these small favors. Conceivably, with veracity and fairness, communication and compromise will be reached. If there is discussion, there will probably be concurrence.

Criticism establishes low self-esteem and a lack of effort. Everyone has various abilities in a myriad of areas. Judging a child sets them up for failure. It also robs them of their confidence and aptitudes. Focus should always be placed on the positive aspects of a child's strengths. A daughter-in-law relishes promising comments and praise of her child. Compliments stimulate greater achievement.

> "Where there is great love, there are always miracles."
>
> Willa Carter

Comparisons of any kind result in uncertainty and mistrust of the person doing the contrasting. Evidence suggests this unsettles a child's motivation and may even advance his or her hesitancy. Most often, appraisals are subjective, immaterial, distorted, and cause devastation of self-esteem. Diversity makes life more interesting.

Disciplining is the daughter-in-law's domain. Small exceptions might be made for mothers-in-law who babysit. A mother-in-law may discipline only with

> "To see things in the seed, that is genius."
>
> Lao-tzu

permission from her daughter-in-law. If the grandmother is supervising the child for any length of time, she may be granted approval to castigate within the realm of reason. The grandmother deserves to be respected and obeyed. The grandmother should be wary of inflicting her views and attitudes toward child rearing onto her grandchildren. The mother-in-law might have to compromise her convictions if they differ from her daughter-in-law's.

> "If I'd known grandchildren were going to be so much fun, I'd had them first."
>
> Anonymous

A daughter-in-law who is too strict will inspire a mother-in-law to investigate ways to circumspect her authority. This is not in good standing, but it could happen to the detriment of all. A daughter-in-law will not easily forgive a mother-in-law's transgressions. This destroys the bonds of faith between the two women. As a result, a mother-in-law may see less of her grandchildren. Most mothers-in-law enjoy their grandchildren. They crave sharing time with them. Sometimes a daughter-in-law unwittingly places obstacles in her mother-in-law's way, preventing a solid union between the mother-in-law and her grandchildren. Supporting her daughter-in-law will ultimately secure her a better chance of cooperation.

Babysitter

A mother-in-law who is not working outside of the home should not automatically become the designated full-time baby-sitter. The mother-in-law who refuses to babysit for her grandchildren is not necessarily uncaring and unloving toward them. This may be so far from the truth but impossible to explain. If a mother-in-law chooses to babysit, that is acceptable. Generalizing about a mother-in-law's culpability when she declines to babysit is improper. Our children are our own responsibility.

Appreciation

Sadly, it appears acknowledging kindness is becoming obsolete. Many people expect favors from others without gratitude. Unwittingly, we may refrain from accepting any obligations from these kindnesses.

We relish our accomplishments, but refuse to recognize the aid given to us from others. We downgrade the huge assistance and influence of others. Grandparents guide and impress our precious children. They most often have profound effects. Grandparents undoubtedly deserve our most laudable acclaim.

"To dream of the person you would like to be is to waste the person you are."

Unknown

Mothers-in-law have a life outside of their children and grandchildren. It is essential to request their services in advance. When we solicit them early, we are conceding their worth.

Disciplining

Although disciplining is within the realm of the parents, as stated previously, exceptions should be made when the mother-in-law is the designated long-term baby-sitter. Parents might conceivably have so many restrictions for their children that a grandparent may feel more like the warden. Grandparents should be able to administer some directions. Trusting your mother-in-law to baby-sit assumes confidence in her supervisory skills.

If the children are at their grandparent's home, certain rules may be enforced that are not imposed at home. The criterion at Grandma's house might be to refrain from jumping on furniture, eating in any room other than the kitchen, helping oneself to food, and banging on furniture with toys. It is practical in this babysitting situation for the daughter-in-law and mother-in-law to be flexible.

> *"It ain't what a man don't know that makes him a fool, but what he does know that ain't so."*
>
> Josh Billings

Methods

Value should be allocated to your mother-in-law's dated approach. Every new advance on the market is not necessarily better. Even if it is improved, some understanding of past techniques will bridge the gap between the newer procedure. Familiarity breeds acceptance. Most of us are comfortable with what we are acquainted. One day, the current methods will also be regarded as obsolete. This helps validate our mother-in-law's approach. Compromising and integrating our assorted ideas promotes admirable models for our children and grandchildren to imitate, so be what you want them to be.

RESPECT

Respect is of great magnitude and extremely valuable. Children will take their cue from their parents. If parents do not show respect for the grandparents, then children will not. This is a situation where you cannot tell your children to do as I say but not as I do. You are the role models. Young children will tune into any degrading remarks you might make about their grandmother. If you cannot say something nice about their grandmother, say nothing at all. Again research suggests that mothers-in-law dislike when children talk back and refuse to follow a given direction. Although parents want their children to speak up for their rights and beliefs, grandma is not the person on which to test these attitudes. Respect also carries over into the realm of refraining from flopping on furniture that was not meant to be sat on. This is simply respect of another's property. A daughter-in-law has more access to disciplining approaches for her children. She can facilitate good behavior through this access. A mother-in-law has no options for dealing with poor behavior and must accept, ignore or tolerate it. A daughter-in-law should step in and handle an irritating issue for the well-being of her mother-in-law. A mother-in-law should not provoke poor behavior from her grand-children. Antagonism will set your grandchildren further apart from you.

1st Vignette

Isaac and Gracie had two children, Christopher who was five and Kelly who was seven. Gracie prized herself with knowledge about the latest modes of child-rearing practices. Emphasis was placed on reading to your child, and this is what Gracie did every night. Gracie's children were involved in a variety of activities, as she desired to keep their minds and bodies active.

> "Children require guidance and sympathy far more than instruction."
>
> Anne Sullivan.

Gracie's mother-in-law, Cheri, frowned on all of this. She believed in instinct and one's natural ability to care for their children. Cheri would make comments about Jeremy's manners or Kelly's constant interruptions. Gracie was disposed to be defensive.

When Cheri was watching the children for Gracie one day, she received the usual instructions upon the children's arrival. The children were to have no candy or desserts. They were to watch no television. Cheri was agitated, but said nothing. She contemplated how to circumvent Gracie's stipulations. Cheri had not been feeling well, and she planned on presenting a movie for her grandchildren. Cheri yearned to see her grandchildren and did not want to mention her infirmities, fearing Gracie would not allow the children to stay. Gracie's last words were no television. Cheri did not fancy playing any board games with them because she had a horrific headache from her sinuses.

Cheri called her friend Lilly, who invited Cheri and the children to come over right away. Lilly loved to see Christopher and Kelly. Lilly immediately offered them two chocolate-chip cookies. Lilly then proceeded to make the children an ice cream cone. With wide grins, the children finished their ice cream in record time. Shortly after, Cheri brought the children back to her own house and waited for Gracie's return.

"Love is a fruit in season at all times, and within reach of every hand".

Mother Teresa

The children never mentioned the cookies or the ice cream. While preparing the children for bed, Gracie helped Christopher out of his shirt. Gracie noticed brown spots on Christopher's shirt. Christopher confessed to the cookies and ice cream. Cheri disparaged the visit as inconsequential. Gracie was aware of the distance to Lilly's house and the necessity of a car ride and the use of seat belts. She also knew Cheri lacked respect for seat belts. Cheri stated quickly that she had put them both in seat belts as the children nodded in agreement.

Gracie retreated with her children for home. She declined Cheri's offer for tea or coffee. Cheri rolled her eyes. Cheri wondered how long it would take

Gracie to recover from this incident. Cheri shrugged. She reasoned when Gracie needed a babysitter she would be called again.

1st Discussion

There are a multitude of challenges in this situation. We might all agree that seat belts are essential. The consumption of cookies and ice cream is arguable. Cheri created a lot of problems for herself unnecessarily. Cheri inadvertently lost Gracie's trust with just cause: Cheri casually violated Gracie's criterion and authority. Gracie might find it difficult to trust Cheri again. It was not Cheri's option to obey or disobey. Gracie questioned if Cheri jeopardized the children's safety.

> "Children are a great comfort in your old age and they help you reach it faster, too."
>
> Lionel Kauffman

Some of Gracie's orders are probably extreme. Cheri is never granted any allowances to coddle her grandchildren. Because she has no clout, Cheri resourcefully circumvents Gracie's authority. This is detrimental to the children and the mother-in-law and daughter-in-law relationship. A daughter-in-law, who is strict, encourages others, including her mother-in-law, to resort to innovative ways to pamper the children. In Cheri's case it was extreme.

It is impractical for Gracie to assume that Cheri must give individual attention to the grandchildren all of the time. Christopher and Kelly received constant attention from their parents and grandparents. They would have had no problem and might have relished amusing themselves. They had all of their activities planned for them, and they were involved in many. As a result, Cheri felt compelled to entertain the children when they were visiting, but she was never sure how to pursue this endeavor.

By virtue of her actions, Cheri did not earn Gracie's confidence. Gracie can feasibly loosen some of the unessential obligations she places on Cheri. This could conceivably ensure an honorable exchange will be procured.

> *"If you were a parent, would you like to be the child of a parent just like you are?"*
>
> Herbert Prochnow

Perhaps we all hold our own paradigms to be true. Mutually blending our convictions weaves truths we could possibly all abide by.

2nd Vignette

Katy dreaded the visits to her mother-in-law's house. Andy, her husband, was close to his mother. He never seemed to understand why Katy was nervous and anxious around her. Andy would just grin and say, "Ignore her."

Katy could not disregard Marie's remarks, especially when it involved their seven-year-old son, Sean. During their last encounter, Marie lectured Katy about Sean's temper. Katy's opinion was that Sean needed time to mature. Hopefully, she thought, Sean would outgrow his petulance or learn to control it. Katy and

Sean had not visited since the dreadful incident. Katy was not looking forward to the inevitable clash.

Katy collected her family and they climbed into the car and drove to Marie's house for dinner. The ride took about an hour. Katy was relieved that she didn't live any closer to Marie. While in the car, Katy gave Sean a long list of instructions regarding appropriate behavior. Sean kept nodding, and Katy sighed. In a short while, they arrived at Marie's house. Andy parked the car, and Katy gestured one last reminder to Sean before proceeding up the walkway.

> "The hardest thing for any young couple to learn is that other parents have perfect children also."
>
> Herbert Prochnow

Marie kissed all of them at the front door and guided them into the den as she always did. When it was time to eat, Sean raced to a chair next to the dessert. As he dragged his finger across the cake a third time, Marie requested Sean move to the other end of the table. Sean frowned and banged his chair as he struggled out of it. Katy anticipated Marie's reaction. Marie had observed the commotion, but said nothing. Observing Sean's dirty hands, Marie asked Sean to go to the sink and scrub his hands for dinner. Sean complained he had already cleaned them. Again, Katy remained silent. The battle ensued.

Katy intercepted Sean, scooping him into her arms. She hugged him till he giggled. Marie watched, resentful of this uncorrected insolence. Sean was laughing, and his anger was gone. Marie projected an angry look at Katy, but remained silent. Katy sent Sean to the bathroom to wash for dinner. Katy avoided Marie's eyes, dreading the consequences of her actions.

Sean was uninterested in eating his food. He opted to spread his vegetables around his plate. Marie always emphasized the importance of an empty dish. That night was no exception. Marie reiterated there would be no dessert if dinner was not finished, although Marie had already wrapped a large piece of cake for Sean to take home. Marie did not care if you were five or ninety-five. You were supposed to have an empty bowl. Marie began removing the dishes from the table. She did not pick up Sean's plate. When the table was wiped, Marie produced a chocolate cake. Sean asked for a piece. Relinquishing her original terms, Marie stated he could have some when he completed some of his supper.

> "The most important thing a father can do for his children is to love their mother."
>
> Theodore M. Hesburgh

Sean complained, but Katy whispered in his ear and he stopped eating and put his fork down. Katy requested a slice of cake. She consumed a small portion of the dessert. Katy gave the remaining piece of cake to Sean. "Thanks, Mom," Sean said as he devoured the cake. Marie said nothing. She loudly slid her chair backward and hastened to the kitchen. Marie had spent a long time making that cake for Sean. Tears welled up in her eyes.

> "Anger is never without a reason but seldom a good one."
>
> Ben Franklin

Marie clanged the dirty dishes together on top of the counter. She declined Katy's offer to help. A short while later, Katy stated she had a headache and would be going home. Katy's good-byes were curt. Marie did not encourage them to stay. Andy was displeased with the abrupt departure. They rode home in silence. Andy gripped the wheel, engrossed in driving. Katy sensed Andy's alienation. At that moment, Sean complained that he had to go to the bathroom. Andy abruptly retorted with finality that Sean could wait. Katy was infuriated. Averting Andy, she glanced out of the passenger's window until they pulled into their driveway. Katy concluded that it was another burdensome visit with the in-laws.

2nd Discussion

Hostility and rage are bursting at the seams. Sean is not the only one displaying fury. It seems that many of

> "All kids are gifted some just open their packages earlier than others."
>
> Michael Carr

the adults lack composure and tranquility. In this situation, Sean is the focal point of the dispute. His mother and grand-mother are struggling to impose their own theories and practices on each other, and Sean is the

226

one who is being manipulated. Sean would be influenced to a greater degree by good behavior.

Andy, Sean's father, is on the fringe of the discord and not aware of the extent of the dispute. He is full of frustration and annoyance and directs it at Sean. Sean is a little boy who is in need of guidance, love, understanding, good role models, and rules.

The mother-in-law and daughter-in-law in this example require an interpretation of their feelings and viewpoints. Neither woman is aware of the other's point of view. The confrontations are escalating, and Katy is encountering relentless agony when visiting her mother-in-law. Marie, on the other hand, is experiencing the same anxieties in addition to the workload involved with the meal. Marie feels powerless to have any authority, even in her own home. She would like to be able to indulge her grandchild with a piece of cake, even if he needs to take it home. Marie would feel she taught Sean the lesson of not wasting food, yet she still wanted him to be able to enjoy his cake because she made it for him.

> "Anger is always more harmful than the insult that caused it".
>
> Chinese Proverb

Katy has not challenged her mother-in-law, nor has she discussed it with her husband. Katy releases her rage through passive-aggressive tactics. It appears she undermines her mother-in-law. Katy does not presume she is sabotaging her mother-in-law's authority, yet she is confounding her endlessly.

Marie is weighed under the subversion. She attempts to assemble a delectable meal, hoping to please her son, grandson, and daughter-in-law. She senses her daughter-in-law's disapproval as soon as Katy walks in the door. Marie knows deep down Katy is anxious to leave every time she looks at her watch. No matter how hard she tries, she never seems to be able to make it a happy time. She's out of ideas and ready to throw in the towel. It's becoming too much work, anxiety, and frustration with nothing to counterbalance these feelings. Marie succeeds in pleasing no one. She cares about her grandson, which is why she is concerned he be instructed in what she considers good manners. This, however, is not her role. Marie disapproves of Katy's disciplining, but her aggressive chastisements are causing friction with her grandson and daughter-in-law.

> "There are two lasting bequests we can give our children: one is roots, the other is wings."
>
> Hodding Carter Jr

If Katy does not attempt to reprove Sean's insolence to his grandmother and her wishes, she will unwittingly destroy Sean's bond with his grandmother. It appears Sean has manifested skill at disregarding his grandmother's wishes. Sean is most likely aware of how to exploit adults for the things he wants. Katy does not comprehend the possibility that Marie loves or cares for Sean. Katy is most often enmeshed in the bickering and criticisms. She has tunnel vision and goes to Marie's prepared for battle. Sean, as a result, is being deprived of his grandmother's love and positive attention.

It is reasonable to assume that Marie's controlling attitude toward Sean is causing friction with her grandson and daughter-in-law. She is possibly scolding Sean so much that Sean is not going to relish excursions to his grandmother's. Marie will never teach Sean anything by her constant disapproval and negative feedback. Marie's reprimands to Sean should be administered sparingly. If Marie feels Sean's behavior necessitates reproach, she might proceed affectionately. It is achievable for Katy to work with Marie to gain the desired results. Marie might have given her mother-in-law the option of allowing Sean to finish half of his dinner and then get the cake. This would have saved face for Marie. It is important for Sean to view his mother and grandmother as a unified front.

> "Anger makes you smaller while forgiveness forces you to grow beyond what you were."
>
> Cherie Carter-Scott

The importance of compromise and collaboration might be reiterated. Those mothers-in-law and daughters-in-law who desire a workable solution might attempt teamwork. The insignificance of winning a small battle versus losing the war cannot be overstated.

Reflections for Mothers-in-Law

Look for the things you have in common with your daughter-in-law. This will help you to bond with each other.

Recognize the power of praise and the debilitation of criticism.

Attempt to empathize with your daughter-in-law. Stop, listen, and reflect.

Heed your daughter-in-law's guidelines for her children and obey them.

Accord your daughter-in-law space to make her own choices regarding the development of her child or children.

React positively to your grandchildren's styles and modes.

Extend equal acceptance of your daughter-in-law's children as well as your daughter's children. This will create positive links for all those involved.

Refrain from comparing your grandchildren. They are all unique individuals, with their own talents and personalities.

Parents are the chief authority figures. Voice an

opinion without forcing your rules.

Give advice only when asked, and keep your advice gentle and minimal.

Reflections for Daughters-in-Law

Remember that your husband is under pressure when you are expecting a baby. Pressure is multiplied for your husband as well as yourself. Recognize his need for acknowledgement.

Display appreciation for favors your mother-in-law does for you. Attempt to return those favors if and when you can.

Accept the differences you and your mother-in-law have in regard to child-development practices.

Tolerate the fact it might not be feasible for your mother-in-law to change her plans when you request a babysitter at the last minute.

Affirm your mother-in-law's desire to express opinions and offer advice. Listen, but use your own judgment.

Allow your mother-in-law visits with the grandchildren. Ties between grandchildren and grandparents are unique and special.

Endeavor to keep babysitting petitions at a reasonable limit.

Confrontations between you and your mother-in-law should be kept quiet and not occur in front of the children.

Explaining your perspectives may help your mother-in-law to understand your approach.

Questions for Daughters-in-Law

1. Do you keep your babysitting requests at a minimum?

   Always   Sometimes   Seldom

2. Have you ever awakened the children if your mother-in-law visits after they are in bed?

   Always   Sometimes   Seldom

3. Does your mother-in-law have some latitude pertaining to decisions for her grandchild, such as offering a cookie?

   Always   Sometimes   Seldom

4. Is your mother-in-law allowed to discipline her grandchild when she is babysitting?

   Always   Sometimes   Seldom

5. Do you trust your mother-in-law to babysit?

   Always   Sometimes   Seldom

6. Do you make your child's restrictions difficult for your mother-in-law to follow?

   Always   Sometimes   Seldom

Questions for Mothers-in-Law

1. Do you sometimes decline to babysit for your daughter-in-law?

   Always   Sometimes   Seldom

2. Do you sabotage your daughter-in-law's restrictions?

   Always   Sometimes   Seldom

3. Do you ever indulge your grandchildren and bend the bedtime rules or food restrictions?

   Always   Sometimes   Seldom

4. Do you compare grandchildren and voice your comparisons?

   Always   Sometimes   Seldom

5. Do you ever stop to question why your daughter-in-law does not trust you?

   Always   Sometimes   Seldom

6. Do you laugh at your daughter-in-law's fears or belittle them?

   Always   Sometimes   Seldom

CONCLUSION

Celebrate you and your mother-in-law. She gave you her son. Celebrate you and your daughter-in-law. She possibly gave you your grandchildren and has made a life with your son. Stand back and think before you speak and remember that when fixations get irritating, there is always a hidden agenda behind the annoyances, whether it's the daughter-in-law's schema or the mother-in-law's, so neither should ever jump to conclusions. When you're having a bad day and you are overlooked for your bad behavior, pay it back through ignoring another's bad day and bad behavior.

Do not compete, compromise. Do not suffer insecurity, have confidence in yourself. Be proud of who you are and be independent. Do not interfere, demonstrate tolerance to each respectively. Accepting another's imperfections allows ours to also be understood.

Recall that jealousy launches the imagination wildly scurrying. Don't let real or imagined jealousies invade your life. It's basically wasted time. Our power resides only with ourselves.

Diplomacy should be used in relationships with others. Respect is key to every action, spoken word, insinuated word, or implied action. Use respect as your thermometer. Keep the negative and unfriendly thoughts and words at a distance and your relationship most likely will improve.

Many lives are here and gone swiftly like a candle softly extinguished. In the course of our lives we will perhaps play both roles being a daughter-in-law and a mother-in-law. Be the kind of daughter-in-law you would want to have. Be the kind of mother-in-law you would want to have. Allow for the uniqueness of our personalities, backgrounds, learning, upbringing, and life's hard lessons along our ways. We really have not walked in another's shoes and will never know the feelings and thoughts and actions they have already experienced before we became an integral part of their lives. We perhaps should think about the tree that survives winter after winter, and storm after storm, and bends all different ways but doesn't break. After many years it doesn't look like the original upright gorgeous tree it once was. It's probably more beautiful because it now has distinctiveness. We are like those trees, ever bending and accommodating to the misfortunes life sends. Please think before you decide to add another upset to your daughter-in-law or to your mother-in-law. Life already sends enough disappointment.

Play fairly and observe with your heart, listen with your heart, speak with your heart and above all else, love totally with all your heart.

"A mother's love is like a circle, it has no beginning and no ending. It keeps going around and around ever expanding, touching everyone who comes in contact with it. Engulfing them like the morning's mist, warming them like the noontime sun, and covering them like a blanket of evening stars. A mother's love is like a circle, it has no beginning and no ending".

Art Urban

"When you were small and just a touch away, I covered you with blankets against the cool night air. But now that you are tall and out of reach. I fold my hands and cover you with prayer"

Dona Madden Cooper.

This is for Mothers and Grandmothers everywhere, trust that there is always love.

Mother-in-law Daughter-in-law Dilemma

ABOUT THE AUTHOR

Pam Reynolds has been writing since the day she was able to pick up a pen. She is the mother of three sons and one daughter, and the mother-in-law of three daughters-in-law and one son-in-law. At present she has five grandchildren, four grandsons and one granddaughter. She currently teaches first grade and in her spare time she enjoys her passion for writing. She has written over twelve children's books as yet unpublished. She is a certified emergency medical technician for over fifteen years, having served as a volunteer on the ambulance in her town of Tolland, for thirteen of those years, and on the Board of Directors for eight. Pam has worked on her book for over fifteen years. In that time her research has led to the conclusions and suggestions entered within the pages of the text. Her main hope is that all who read her book will have a greater understanding and peacefulness in their relationships with their mothers-in-law and daughters-in-law.